Kids' Quilts
in a
Weekend

20 colourful projects suitable
for babies to 10-year-olds

Elizabeth Keevill

hamlyn

To Kevin and Isabelle, with love.

First published in Great Britain in 2004 by
Hamlyn, a division of Octopus Publishing Group Ltd
2–4 Heron Quays, London E14 4JP

ISBN 0 600 60920 0

A CIP catalogue record for this book
is available from the British Library

Printed and bound in China

10 9 8 7 6 5 4 3 2 1

Contents

Introduction

Unlike many favourite toys that are often just a passing fad, a quilt is a gift that a child will treasure for years. Once outgrown as a bed cover, it can be displayed as a wall hanging or may be handed on to the next generation as an heirloom. Quilt-making has a reputation for being a time-consuming craft, involving many hours of close work and endless patience. Today, however, there are modern tools, materials and time-saving tips, which make it possible to produce a quilt in a relatively short space of time.

How to use this book

Kids' Quilts in a Weekend is divided into four sections. The first contains the least complex projects, which can be made up easily in a weekend. The projects in the second section require more effort to complete in a weekend and need a slightly wider range of skills. Section three contains projects for which some advance preparation is necessary as well as greater skill. The fourth section offers information on the materials, equipment, skills and techniques that you will need to complete the projects, even if starting from scratch. Once you have chosen a project, read through the instructions carefully from start to finish to make sure you understand the work involved. Specific materials and equipment are listed and followed by a step-by-step description of how the quilt is assembled.

Working with fabric

Sewing involves repeated handling of the fabric and, unless you take care, material can become grimy very quickly. Wash your hands before you start and never eat while you are working. Cut fabric in batches, or cut out just enough for one session, and store in clear plastic bags. Keep your work in progress clean by storing the whole project – including templates or patterns – in a large plastic bag. Make sure you keep any patchwork pieces flat once they are cut out: ironing them after cutting can cause distortion and may lead to inaccuracies in piecing.

All fabric quantities take into account the width of the fabric and allow a little extra for error. If, however, you are using up scraps of fabric, you may be able to get away with using less.

To avoid wastage, cut the pieces from your fabric as economically as possible: cutting guides have been provided for a number of projects.

All measurements are given in metric with imperial conversions. Where accuracy is vital, the conversions are exact. Otherwise the amounts have been rounded up or down and will not be direct equivalents. For this reason, use either metric or imperial, but do not mix the two.

Safety notes

When making articles for children and babies, it is essential that the materials you use are safe and that you construct the object carefully so as to avoid accidents. In particular:
Make sure the object is carefully sewn and securely finished off so that stuffing, filling and wadding cannot come out, which could cause choking.

Never have quilts dry-cleaned: fumes from the cleaning fluid can remain in the article, which could result in death if the quilt were used on a child's bed.

Scissors, seam rippers, craft knives, needles, pins and rotary cutters can all be very dangerous to small children. Keep all your equipment in a safe place, out of the reach of children, while you are working, and once you have finished a project.

Take note of any age restrictions given in the project. Small items such as buttons, beads and pompoms can be chewed off and must not be used on quilts for children under three years.

Babies can overheat if their bedding is too warm and this may be a contributory factor to cot death, or Sudden Infant Death Syndrome (SIDS). Use only very lightweight quilts on a baby's cot, and only in cooler weather.

Lazy Weekend

In a short space of time you can make a beautiful gift that will be treasured for many years to come.

Here are six basic projects that demonstrate how striking colours and stunning fabrics can be used to make something very simple look truly outstanding. Each project can be completed in a weekend following the simple instructions, once you have assembled the necessary materials and equipment.

Quick & Easy Snuggle Quilt

The finished size of the comforter is approximately 180 x 115cm (71 x 45in), which makes it suitable as a topper for a single bed or a sofa cuddle quilt. The exact size of your finished comforter will depend on the pattern of your chosen fabric and its width.

Filled with high-loft polyester wadding for maximum warmth and cosiness, this easy-to-make comforter will become your child's firm favourite for snuggling on the sofa, as a bed topper or for sleepovers with friends. The fabric is already printed with a patchwork-effect pattern, which allows you to produce a complex-looking quilt in the minimum of time. Choose a simpler, smaller-scale or plain fabric for the backing, in colours that coordinate with the top fabric – we have used pink gingham.

✂ you will need

Fabric quantities assume a width of at least 140cm (55in)
Seam allowance: 1.5cm (⅝in)

- 200cm (79in) patchwork-effect or large-check fabric for the quilt top (exact quantities will depend on the pattern)

- 200cm (79in) pink gingham for the backing (exact quantities will depend on the pattern)

- 190 x 120cm (75 x 47in), 55g (2oz) or 115g (4oz) polyester wadding (batting) (the exact size will depend on your choice of fabric and

the size of the quilt. As a rule, your piece of wadding should be at least the same size as the finished quilt.)

- four bulldog clips, strong clothes pegs or large safety pins for 'bagging out'

- white sewing thread

- pink hand-quilting thread

- see also basic equipment (page 108)

to make the quilt

1 Before you cut your fabric, decide on the exact size of your quilt, taking into account the design of the fabric and ensuring you include complete pattern repeats. Add 3cm (1¼in) both to the width and the length to allow for 1.5cm (⅝in) seams all round and cut a rectangle of fabric to form the top of the quilt (✂ 1). Our quilt top is made from a piece of fabric 183 x 118cm (72 x 46½in).

2 Using the quilt top as your template, cut a rectangle from the pink gingham for the quilt backing.

3 'Bag out' the quilt and insert the wadding following the instructions on page 120.

4 Pin-baste the quilt all over, avoiding the areas where you will be quilting, following the instructions on page 112.

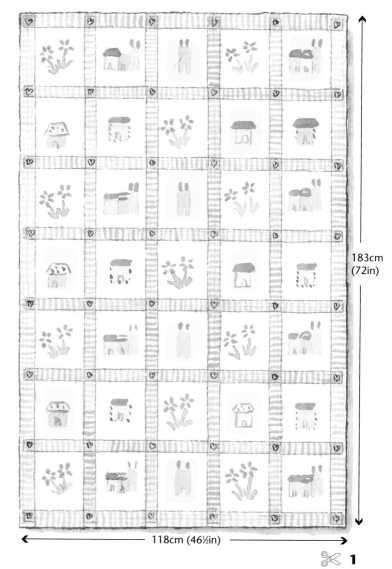

183cm (72in)

118cm (46½in)

✂ **1**

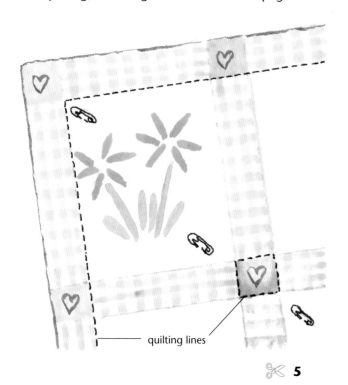

quilting lines

✂ **5**

5 Using pink quilting thread, hand-quilt all round the comforter to form a border about 5cm (2in) from the outer edge. The exact distance will depend on the design of your fabric (✂ 5).

6 Hand-quilt around the central squares in the same way.

Quilting by hand

While not as fast as quilting by machine, this technique has a distinctive quality and, on a quilt this size, does not take long. Hand-quilting is also the better choice for thick quilts such as this one (if you have used 115g (4oz) wadding), which can be tricky to manoeuvre on a machine. If you have used 55g (2oz) wadding you may prefer to machine-quilt (see page 112). If you find it tricky to sew around the central squares by machine, try sewing two sides at a time, cutting the thread and then rotating the quilt by 90 degrees so you can sew the other two sides from the same angle.

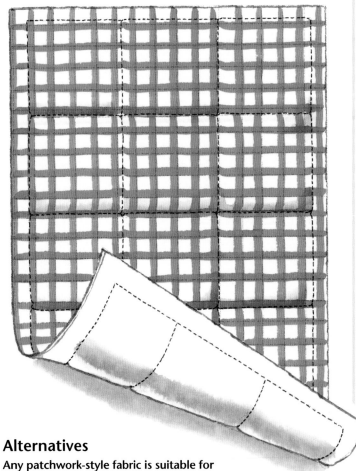

Alternatives

Any patchwork-style fabric is suitable for this project and a large-check fabric would do equally well. The design on the fabric not only provides the guide for the size of the quilt but also a guide for the quilting; the exact pattern of the quilting will therefore vary according to your fabric. In our design, we have hand-quilted around the central squares. You may be able to copy this idea, or a further option is to 'tie' the central panel of the comforter instead of, or in addition to, quilting it by hand (see page 113).

Soft & Tufty Comforter

The finished size of the quilt is approximately 160 x 115cm (63 x 45in). It can be used as a tucked-in cot quilt or as a single-bed topper. Alternatively you could, if you wish, make the quilt larger, in which case you will need to use wider fabric or sheeting or join lengths of fabric together.

This eye-catching and quick-to-make comforter is made from single pieces of 'shot' handwoven fabric with a lively contrasting print for the binding, which was the source of inspiration for the colour scheme. Rather than having stitched quilting, this quilt is tied. The technique is much quicker than sewn quilting and is particularly effective when used in conjunction with high-loft polyester wadding, resulting in a plump, dimpled effect. Futon-style tufts create an interesting random pattern.

✂ you will need

Fabric quantities assume a width of at least 115cm (45in)
Seam allowance 1.5cm (⅝in)

- 160cm (63in) turquoise fabric for the quilt top

- 160cm (63in) orange fabric for the backing

- 80cm (32in) patterned fabric for binding strips

- 165 x 120cm (65 x 47in) good-quality 115g (4oz) bonded polyester wadding (batting)

- light-blue sewing thread

- two skeins primrose-yellow soft embroidery thread

- crewel needle (embroidery needle) with a large eye

- see also basic equipment (page 108)

Note To avoid the danger of choking, do not make the tufts too long, particularly for younger children. Ensure they are tightly and securely knotted and check regularly for fraying or loosening of the threads.

to make the comforter

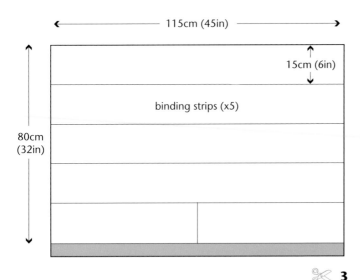

115cm (45in)

15cm (6in)

binding strips (x5)

80cm (32in)

✂ 3

1 Cut a 150 x 106cm (59 x 41¾in) rectangle from the turquoise fabric. Using this as a template, cut the orange backing fabric 4.5cm (1¾in) larger all round than the turquoise fabric. The orange fabric will therefore measure 159 x 115cm (62½ x 45in). Use the orange fabric as a template to cut the wadding to the same size.

2 Lay the orange fabric on the floor, wrong side up (if applicable), spreading it out carefully. Lay the wadding on top, smoothing out any wrinkles, and centre the turquoise fabric on top of the wadding. You should have an even border of wadding visible all round. With the turquoise fabric uppermost, pin-baste the three layers together following the instructions on page 112.

3 Cut five binding strips 15cm (6in) deep from the whole width of the patterned fabric (✂ 1). Cut one of the binding strips in half and join each half to another strip, end-to-end, so that you have two short strips and two long ones. Prepare each strip following the instructions on page 121.

4 Using light-blue sewing thread, bind the edges of the quilt beginning with the short ends, following the instructions on page 122.

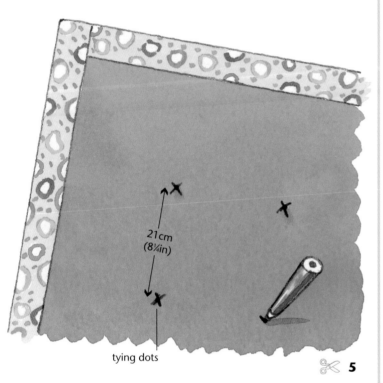

21cm
(8¼in)

tying dots

✂ **5**

5 With the turquoise fabric uppermost, mark tying dots on the surface of the quilt, approximately 21cm (8¼in) apart (✂ 5).

6 Cut 12 pieces of primrose-yellow soft embroidery thread 100cm (39in) long and follow the instructions on page 113 to 'tie' the quilt. Work in horizontal rows and use reef knots. Use sharp scissors to trim the tufts to 1.5cm (⅝in) for children under three years old and up to 5cm (2in) for older children.

Alternatives

You can choose any printed or patterned fabric for the binding and select plain, coordinating colours for the front and back panels. Instead of using one colour of embroidery thread you could use multicoloured thread or fine embroidery ribbon. The quilt can be buttoned (see page 113) or a row of buttons could be added between each row of ties. However, buttons are not suitable for children under three years old.

Powder-coloured Diamonds

Cheerful and summery, this quilt has a bright, geometrical design that is likely to appeal to older children. Large squares are cut from powder-coloured fabrics and arranged diagonally following a traditional arrangement known as 'on point'. The vertical and horizontal quilting lines break up the large diamonds into smaller triangular shapes, while the patterned fabrics add further interest.

The finished size of the quilt is approximately 202 x 148cm (79½ x 58in) making it suitable for use on a standard single bed.

✂ you will need

Fabric quantities assume a fabric width of at
least 150cm (59in) unless stated otherwise*.
Seam allowance 1.5cm (⅝in)

- 70cm (28in) light-blue fabric with darker
  dots

- 70cm (28in) light-pink fabric with darker
  dots

- 70cm (28in) dark-pink fabric

- 70cm (28in) purple-blue fabric

- 70cm (28in) light-blue fabric

- 50cm (20in) light-green fabric

- 50cm (20in) mid-blue fabric

- 50cm (20in) turquoise fabric

- 30cm (12in) jade fabric

- 210cm (83in) blue fabric for backing or
  150cm (59in) of wide-width* sheeting
  (at least 210cm (83in) wide)

- 210 x 150cm (83 x 59in) 55g (2oz)
  polyester wadding (batting)

- light-blue sewing thread

- invisible quilting thread

- see also basic equipment (page 108)

- thin card for the templates, cut as follows:
  23cm (9in) square
  20cm (7¾in) square

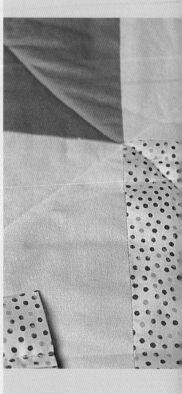

to make the quilt

1 From the light-blue fabric with darker dots cut seven binding strips 11cm (4⅜in) deep by 110cm (59in) wide from across the width of the fabric, then from the remainder of the fabric cut 12 squares using the 23cm (9in) template. Still with the 23cm (9in) template cut the following squares:

- light-pink fabric with darker dots (twelve)
- dark-pink fabric (twelve)
- purple-blue fabric (twelve)
- light-blue fabric (nine)
- light-green fabric (eight)
- mid-blue fabric (eight)
- turquoise fabric (six)
- jade fabric (four)

2 Lay the squares out on the floor in the correct order (✂ 2). Starting at the top left-hand corner, join the squares in each diagonal row taking 1.5cm (⅝in) seams and using a light-blue sewing thread (see instructions on page 110). For accuracy, draw seam lines on the back using the 20cm (7¾in) square and a vanishing marker. Machine-sew, then press the seams open and mark each row with its number (see page 110).

row one, row two, row three, row four, row five, row six, row seven, row eight, row nine, row ten, row eleven, row twelve, row thirteen

✂ **2**

3 Lay out the rows and pin to each other in the correct order, ensuring that you stagger the beginning of each row and that the seams align from row to row (see page 111). Press the seams open.

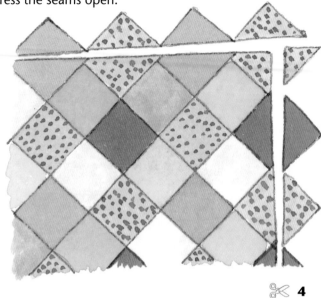

✂ **4**

4 Square off the quilt top by drawing a line 1.5cm (⅝in) further out than an imaginary line that links the points of the diamonds all round the edge of the quilt (✂ 4). Cut along this line to form a rectangular quilt top. The extra 1.5cm (⅝in) is to create a seam allowance around the edge of the quilt for the binding stage.

5 Use the quilt top as a template to cut the blue backing fabric 3cm (1¼in) larger all round. Cut the wadding to the same size as the backing. Lay the backing fabric on the floor, wrong side up (if applicable), spreading it out carefully. Lay the wadding on top, smoothing out any wrinkles, and centre the quilt top on the wadding. You should have an even border of wadding visible all round. With the quilt top uppermost, pin-baste the three layers together following the instructions on page 112.

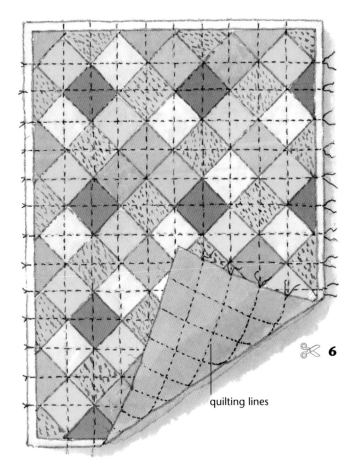

quilting lines

✂ **6**

6 Using invisible quilting thread, quilt in vertical lines, linking the points of the diamonds (✂ 6). Sew in one direction – from top to bottom only – otherwise the quilt will distort. You will need to roll up the right-hand side of the quilt to sew the left-hand lines (see page 113). When you have quilted all the vertical lines, quilt the horizontal lines. To avoid puckering and bunching because you are sewing on the bias (across the weave of the fabric), you will need to stretch the fabric gently at right angles to the quilting line as you go. Place your hands on the fabric on either side of the needle and smooth your hands across the fabric, away from the needle, as you sew.

7 Join two pairs of the binding strips, end-to-end, to form two long strips. Cut one of the remaining binding strips in half and join each half to each of the two other remaining strips in the same way. You will now have two short and two long strips. Prepare each strip following the instructions on page 121.

8 Using light-blue sewing thread, bind the edges of the quilt beginning with the long sides, following the instructions on page 122.

Alternatives
If you have used good-quality bonded polyester wadding you can tie the quilt in the centre of each diamond with a red soft embroidery cotton tie (see page 113). A small cross-stitch where the diamonds intersect would also help to hold the layers in place.

Undersea Laundry Bag

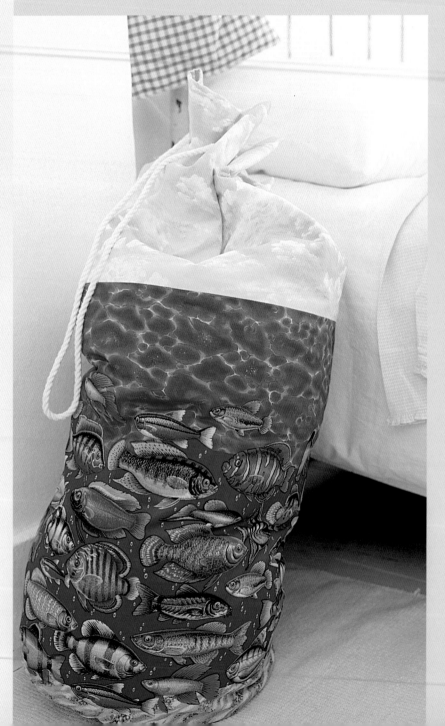

This striking laundry bag is bound to encourage kids to put their dirty clothes away tidily rather than leaving them strewn on the bedroom floor. Relying on a wonderful mixture of novelty fabrics for its effect, the bag has eyelets and rope around the top, which fit with the nautical theme. Pre-wash the fabrics and bond the fish on carefully and you should be able to machine-wash the bag to keep it sweet and fresh.

The finished size of the bag is approximately 90 x 52cm (35½ x 20½in) but you can make it larger or smaller to suit a multitude of purposes.

✂ you will need

Fabric quantities assume a width of at least
110cm (43in) unless stated otherwise*
Seam allowance 1.5cm (⅝in)

- 70cm (28in) sand-and-pebble print fabric

- 40cm (16in) fish-print fabric

- 60cm (24in) sky-print fabric

- 30cm (12in) sea-print fabric

- 120cm (47in) white or light-blue fabric to
  line the bag (sheeting is fine)

- 40cm (16in) firm iron-on interfacing, 91cm
  (36in) wide*

- 120cm (47in) fusible webbing, 46cm (18in)
  wide*

- light-blue, white and sand-coloured sewing
  threads

- 105cm (41in) light-weight iron-on wadding
  (batting), 89cm (35in) wide*

- 20cm (8in) cm soft iron-on interfacing,
  91cm (36in) wide*

- ten x 1.4mm (½in) eyelets and fixing tool

- 150cm (59in) cotton or nylon rope, max.
  1cm or (⅜in) diameter (ask for the ends of
  the rope to be sealed)

- see also basic equipment (page 108)

- paper for the templates, cut as follows:
  36.5cm (14⅜in) diameter circle
  33.5cm (13³⁄₁₆in) diameter circle

Note As the bag has rope threaded in it, it
should not be given to children under three
years old or left within their reach.

to make the laundry bag

1 With the sand-and-pebble fabric spread out widthways, cut a 36.5cm (14⅜in) diameter circle from the top corner and trim the remaining fabric across the width to make a rectangle measuring 110 x 33.5 cm (43 x 13³⁄₁₆in). Cut two 33.5cm (13³⁄₁₆in) diameter circles from the firm interfacing. Iron one to the centre of the wrong side of the fabric circle you have just cut and reserve the other one for later.

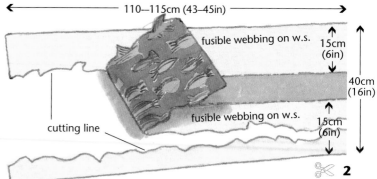

110–115cm (43–45in)

fusible webbing on w.s.   15cm (6in)

40cm (16in)

cutting line

fusible webbing on w.s.   15cm (6in)

✂ **2**

2 Cut two strips of fusible webbing 15cm (6in) deep and same width as the fish fabric. Press the webbing to the top and bottom edges of the wrong side of the fish fabric, according to the webbing manufacturer's instructions. Following the shapes of the fish and keeping as near as possible to the centre line of each webbing section, cut around the fish using small scissors (✂ 2). This should give you a shaped edge, top and bottom. Cut out any complete fish shapes from the fabric remnants and put to one side.

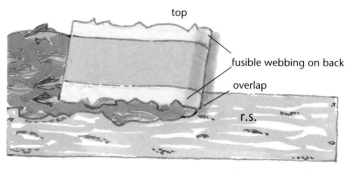

top

fusible webbing on back

overlap

r.s.

✂ **2**

3 Lay the sand-and-pebble fabric out widthways, right side up. Place the fish fabric panel above it, right side up, with the fish the correct way up. Slide the fish fabric over the sand fabric until the top edge of the fusible webbing on the lower part of the fish fabric lines up exactly with the top edge of the sand fabric (✂ 3). (You can place pins at the edge of the webbing to help you overlap the fabrics accurately.) Fuse the fabrics together following the manufacturer's instructions.

4 Lay the sea fabric out widthways, right side up. Place the top edge of the fish fabric over the bottom edge of the sea fabric and, as before, position the area of fusible webbing so the edge of the sea fabric coincides with the edge of the webbing. Fuse together.

5 Bond the reserved cut-out fish the correct way up onto the sea and sand-and-pebble areas.

6 The total height of the three pieces of bonded fabric should be approximately 56cm (22in). If it is much more than this, trim the sea and sand fabrics carefully in a straight line at a right angle to the selvage.

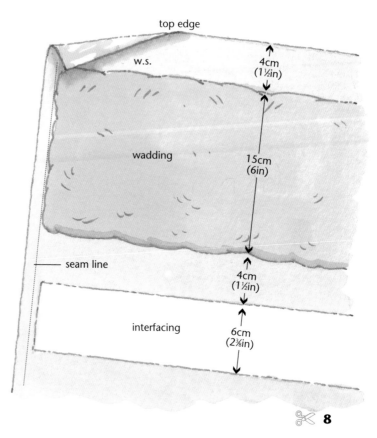

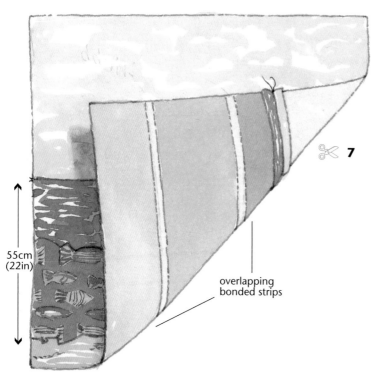

7 Using light-blue sewing thread, sew the sky fabric to the top edge of the sea fabric, taking a 1.5cm (⅝in) seam (✂ 7). Press the seam open.

8 Cut a 15cm (6in) strip off one long edge of the iron-on wadding. Put the rest of the wadding to one side. Working on the wrong side of the sky fabric, position the top edge of this strip 4cm (1½in) down from the top edge of the sky fabric, starting and finishing just short of the seam lines (✂ 8). Iron in place following the manufacturer's instructions. From the whole width of the soft iron-on interfacing, cut two 6cm (2⅜in) deep strips. Place the strips of interfacing end-to-end across the width of the fabric, leaving a 4cm (1½in) gap below the wadding strip, and starting just short of the left-hand seam line (✂ 8). You will need to trim the end of the second piece just short of the right-hand seam line. Iron in place following the manufacturer's instructions.

9 To make the bag, fold the fabric in half lengthways, right sides together, and pin the short edges to form a tube, matching up the sea/sky seams. Machine-stitch the seams using light-blue sewing thread and press them open, but leave the tube inside out.

10 Take the sand fabric circle, fold it exactly into four and mark small dots in the seam allowance to indicate the quarters. Open it out. Fold the tube into four (ignoring the seam allowance) and mark the quarters with small dots in the seam allowance at the bottom of the tube. Open it out. Pin the circle to bottom of the tube, matching up the dots. Be sure to pin the seam line of the tube to the seam line of the base (rather than the raw edges of each), otherwise they won't fit. Machine-sew around the seam line of the base using sand-coloured sewing thread. Snip the seam allowance of the base but do not cut right up to the stitches (✂ 10).

w.s.

cutting lines

sewing line

base

✂ **10**

11 Cut a rectangle of lining fabric 108 x 77cm (42½ x 30¼in). Lay the lining fabric out flat and centre the rest of the wadding on it. There should be a narrow margin of fabric extending all round the edge. Iron the wadding onto the fabric, following the manufacturer's instructions.

12 Pin the longer sides of the lining fabric together to form a tube and sew along the seam, leaving a 20cm (8in) gap in the middle. Use light-blue or white sewing thread, depending on the colour of the lining fabric. Press the seam open. Cut a 36.5cm (14⅜in) circle of lining fabric and centre the reserved 33.5cm (13³⁄₁₆in) diameter circle of firm interfacing on the wrong side. Iron in place following the manufacturer's instructions. Sew the circle to one end of the lining tube, following the instructions in step 10.

13 Turn the lining inside out, so that the raw edges are on the inside. With the outer bag also turned inside out, place the lining bag inside the outer bag. The right sides of both bags should be together. Line up the side seams and pin the two bags together along the top edge, with raw edges level. The base of the lining will be higher than the base of the outer bag (✂ 13). Machine-sew along the seam line at the top of the bags using light-blue sewing thread.

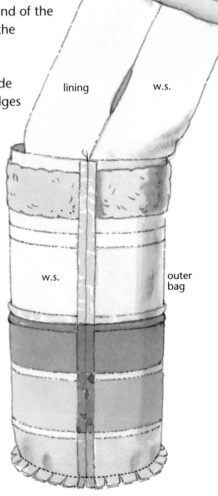

lining   w.s.

w.s.   outer bag

✂ **13**

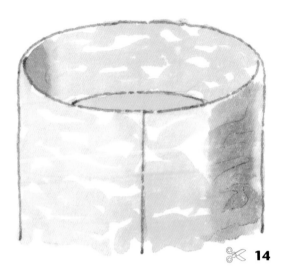

✂ **14**

14 Pull the outer bag out through the opening in the lining and turn both parts right sides out. Oversew (see page 117) or machine-stitch (by pinching the edges together) the gap in the lining. Use light-blue or white sewing thread depending on the colour of the lining fabric. Push the lining bag down inside the outer bag so the base circles lie on top of each other – now there should be about 18cm (7in) of sky fabric on the inside of the upper part of the bag (✂ 14). Press the top edge of the bag to form a sharp crease.

15 Turn the whole bag inside out. Using a vanishing marker or tailor's chalk, mark a line all round the inside of the bag, 7cm (2¾in) from the top edge. On the line, mark a dot 5cm (2in) to one side of the seam. Starting at this point, measure off every 10.5cm (4⅛in) along the line, marking a dot on the line each time. You should have ten dots. Adjust the positions slightly if they do not work out exactly the same distance apart. These dots are the positions for your eyelets.

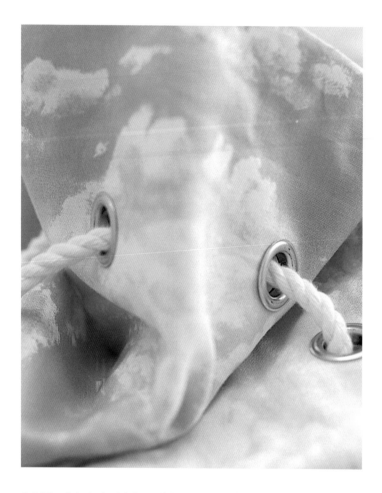

16 The fabric is thick at this point so the hole-cutter supplied with eyelet kits may not work. Instead, draw round the inside of one of the eyelet backing rings, centred on each dot and, using small sharp scissors, carefully snip out the holes through all layers. It is a good idea to practise fitting the eyelets on a scrap of fabric before you embark on the actual bag.

17 Turn the bag the correct way round and fit the eyelets through the holes following the manufacturer's instructions. Thread the rope through the eyelets and knot each end.

Checkers Sleepover Quilt

The finished size of the quilt is approximately 185 x 120cm (73 x 47in) – a good size for a bed topper on a standard single bed.

Perfect for sleepovers, this quilt is not just for sleeping under, but also forms a giant draughts (checkers) board and comes complete with soft playing pieces. There is even a bag to put them in. Midnight feasts will never be the same again! We use a short cut for making the black-and-white checks for this quilt, which speeds up the piecing and makes the project easy to achieve in a weekend.

✂ you will need

Fabric quantities assume a width of at least 110cm (43in)
Seam allowance 1.5cm (⅝in)

- 180cm (71in) black fabric

- 180cm (71in) white fabric

- 170cm (67in) red fabric

- 200cm (79in) coordinating fabric for the backing

- black, red and white sewing threads

- 200 x 120cm (79 x 47in) 55g (2oz) polyester wadding (batting)

- invisible quilting thread

- 250g (10oz) soft polyester toy stuffing

- 100cm (39in) no. 4 white cotton piping cord, or similar thin rope

- see also basic equipment (page 108)

- thin card or acetate and paper for the templates, cut as follows:
  14cm (5½in) square (cut from card or acetate)
  68 x 17cm (26½in x 6¾in) rectangle (cut from paper)

to make the quilt

1 Cut the black, white and red fabrics according to the cutting guides (✂ 1a, 1b and 1c).

2 Take four each of the black and white checker strips and pin them, long edges together, with a seam allowance of 1.5cm (⅝in). Alternate the colours to form a rectangle of black-and-white stripes. Repeat with the remaining four checker strips to form another rectangle. Sew along the seam lines using white sewing thread and press all seams open (✂ 2).

3 Using the paper rectangle template as a guide, divide each rectangle into four 17cm (6¾in) deep strips, cutting at right angles to the seam lines (✂ 2). Reverse every other strip then pin and sew to form two checker rectangles. Press the seams open. Arrange the two rectangles so that contrasting squares abut and sew together to form a checker square using white sewing thread (✂ 3).

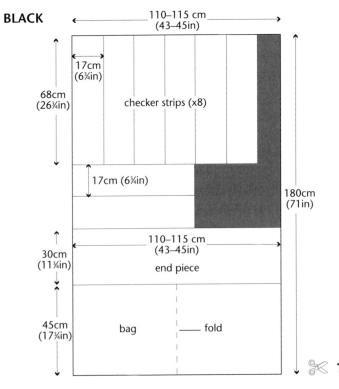

BLACK

110–115 cm (43–45in)

17cm (6¾in)

68cm (26¾in)

checker strips (x8)

17cm (6¾in)

180cm (71in)

110–115 cm (43–45in)

end piece

30cm (11¾in)

45cm (17¾in)

bag — fold

✂ **1a**

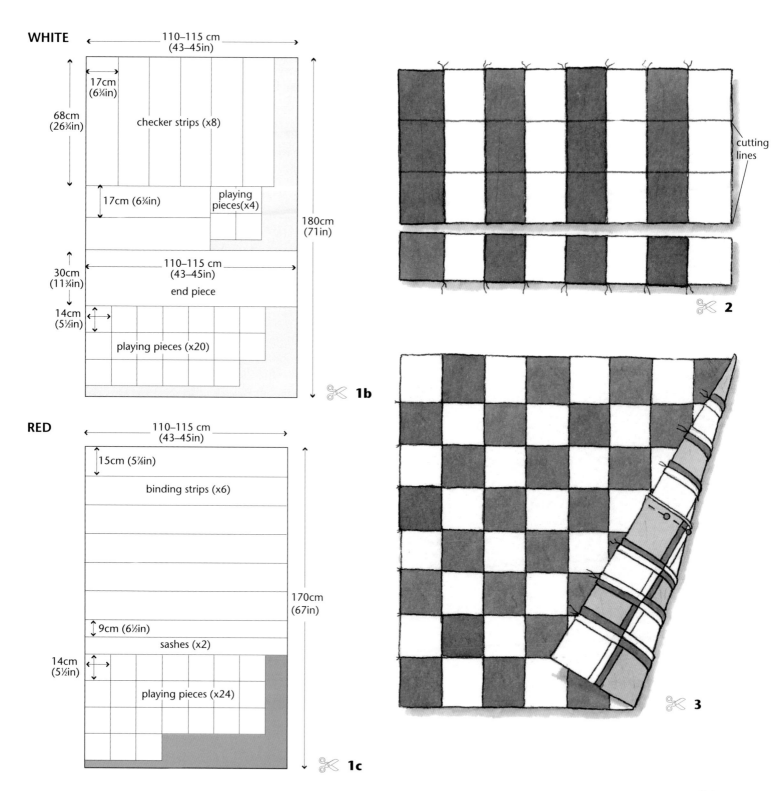

WHITE

110–115 cm
(43–45in)

17cm
(6¾in)

68cm
(26¾in)

checker strips (x8)

17cm (6¾in)

playing
pieces(x4)

180cm
(71in)

110–115 cm
(43–45in)

30cm
(11¾in)

end piece

14cm
(5½in)

playing pieces (x20)

✂ **1b**

cutting
lines

✂ **2**

RED

110–115 cm
(43–45in)

15cm (5⅞in)

binding strips (x6)

170cm
(67in)

9cm (6½in)

sashes (x2)

14cm
(5½in)

playing pieces (x24)

✂ **1c**

✂ **3**

14cm
(5½in)

quilting lines

✂ 4

6 Lay the backing fabric on the floor, wrong side up (if applicable), and lay the wadding on top. Centre the quilt top on last, right side up, with an even margin of wadding extending all round. Pin-baste through all layers, avoiding any seam lines, following the instructions on page 112.

7 Using tailor's chalk on the black fabric and vanishing marker on the white fabric, mark quilting lines on the end pieces 14cm (5½in) apart (✂ 4). These are a continuation of the vertical checker lines. Machine-quilt along the lines using black thread on the black fabric and white on the white fabric, stopping at the red sashes and reversing the stitch for a few stitches to fasten off.

8 Using invisible quilting thread in the top of your machine and white in the bobbin, 'stitch-in-the-ditch' along all other seam lines (see page 112).

9 Take four of the red binding strips and join them to form two long strips. You now have two short strips and two long ones. Prepare each strip following the instructions on page 121.

10 Using red sewing thread, bind the edges of the quilt starting with the short sides, following the instructions on page 122.

4 Take the two narrower red sash strips and pin to the top and bottom of the checker square, right sides facing, raw edges level. Ensure that the squares at the bottom right- and top left-hand corners are white. Machine-stitch using red sewing thread and taking a 1.5cm (⅝in) seam. Press the seam open (✂ 4). Take the black and white end pieces. Pin and sew these onto the red sash strips and press the seams open.

5 Spread the backing fabric on the floor and smooth it out carefully. Using the quilt top as a template, cut the backing fabric 4cm (1½in) bigger all round. Cut the wadding to the same size as the backing fabric.

11 For the playing pieces, pin the 14cm (5½in) squares of fabric in pairs, right sides together. Sew all round with a 1.5cm (⅝in) seam allowance, leaving a 7.5cm (3in) gap in one side for turning and stuffing (✂ 11).

14cm (5½in)

1.5cm (⅝in)

7.5cm (3in) gap

sewing line

✂ 11

12 Trim the corners of each square (✂ 12) and turn right sides out, poking out the corners very gently with a closed pair of sewing scissors. Press the squares and fill each one with polyester toy stuffing until it is puffy but not hard. Oversew the opening with the appropriate coloured sewing thread using small, neat stitches (see page 117).

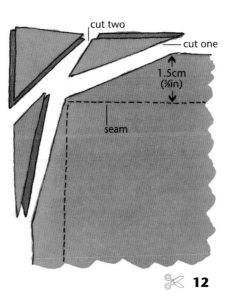

cut two
cut one
1.5cm (⅝in)
seam
✂ 12

13 Take the rectangle of fabric for the bag and fold it in half along the short fold, right sides facing (if applicable). Press along this line. Sew the side seams. If the fabric seems prone to fray, neaten the raw edges of the side seams by pressing under a small turning on each edge and machining into

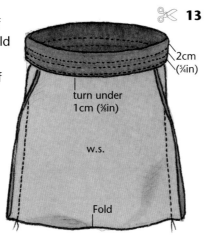

✂ 13
2cm (¾in)
turn under 1cm (⅜in)
w.s.
Fold

place. Press the seams open. With the bag still inside out, turn the top edge of the bag under 1cm (⅜in) to the wrong side and machine-sew in place. Fold the top of the bag down a further 6cm (2⅜in) to the wrong side. Machine two lines of stitching all the way around the top of the bag, 2cm (¾in) and 4cm (1½in) from the top fold (✂ 13).

14 Turn the bag right sides out. Unpick the stitching in both side seams between the stitching lines on the outside of the bag. Thread the cord through attached to a safety pin. Knot each end of the cord and use the bag for storing the playing pieces (✂ 14).

✂ 14

Rainbow Quilt

The vibrant colours and prints used for this quilt make the project look far more complex than it is – in fact it is as basic as patchwork can be! We have used four bright prints plus single-coloured marbled fabrics in deep-blue, yellow, lime green, apple green, red, deep-red, bright pink, orange and sky blue, but you can use fewer colours if you wish. Placing the bright fabrics and prints next to contrasting colours intensifies their effect.

The finished size of the quilt is approximately 125 x 100cm (49 x 39in), which will fit a standard cot. Alternatively, you can use the quilt as a wall hanging or scale it up to fit a large cot or single bed.

✄ you will need

Fabric quantities assume a width of at least
110cm (43in) wide
Seam allowance 1.5cm (⅝in)

- 130cm (51in) red fabric for the backing

- 80cm (32in) fabric printed with diagonal rainbow stripes for the binding and squares

- at least nine fat quarters of various clear bright marbles and prints. We used the following quantities for this quilt:
  40cm (16in) circles-print fabric
  40cm (16in) spectrum-print fabric
  40cm (16in) lime-green marbled fabric
  20cm (8in) orange-and-yellow striped fabric
  20cm (8in) yellow marbled fabric
  20cm (8in) bright-pink marbled fabric
  20cm (8in) deep-blue marbled fabric

20cm (8in) apple-green marbled fabric
20cm (8in) sky-blue marbled fabric
20cm (8in) orange marbled fabric
20cm (8in) red marbled fabric
20cm (8in) deep-red marbled fabric

- neutral-coloured and red sewing threads

- 125 x 100cm (49 x 39in) 55g (2oz) polyester wadding (batting)

- invisible quilting thread

- see also basic equipment (page 108)

- acetate for the templates, cut as follows:
  15cm (6in) square
  12cm (4¾in) square

to make the quilt

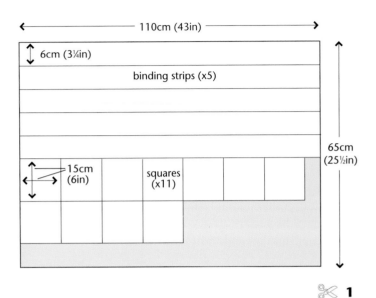

1 Follow the cutting guide (✂ 1) to cut five 6cm (3¼in) deep strips from the width of the binding fabric, and eleven 15cm (6in) squares.

2 Using the 15cm (6in) square template, cut the following number of squares from each fabric (listed in brackets). If you want to follow a design of your own, cut eighty squares from your chosen fabrics – you should be able to cut nine squares from a fat quarter:

- circles-print fabric (eight)
- spectrum-print fabric (eight)
- lime-green marbled fabric (eight)
- orange-and-yellow striped fabric (seven)
- yellow marbled fabric (seven)
- bright-pink marbled fabric (seven)
- deep-blue marbled fabric (six)
- apple-green marbled fabric (four)
- sky-blue marbled fabric (four)
- orange marbled fabric (four)
- red marbled fabric (three)
- deep-red marbled fabric (three)

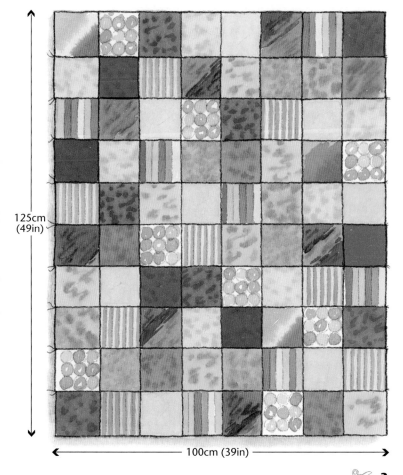

125cm (49in)

100cm (39in)

✂ **3**

4 Following the instructions on page 110, join the squares in each row taking 1.5cm (⅝in) seams and using a neutral-coloured sewing thread. For accuracy, draw seam lines on the back using the 12cm (4¾in) square and a vanishing marker. Machine-sew, then press the seams open. Mark the row number on each left-hand square.

5 Join the rows together, ensuring they are in the correct order and that the seams of each row align (see page 111). Press the seams open.

6 Use the quilt top to cut the red backing fabric 1cm (⅜in) bigger all round than the quilt top. Cut the wadding to the same size as the backing fabric.

7 Lay the backing fabric on the floor wrong side up (if applicable), lay the wadding on top, and centre the quilt top on that. There should be an even border of wadding all round. Pin-baste the three layers together, avoiding the seam lines, following the instructions on page 112.

8 Using invisible thread in the top of your machine and red thread in the bobbin quilt along all seam lines by stitching-in-the-ditch (see page 112).

9 Take the 8cm (3¼in) deep binding strips. Cut one into two equal lengths and sew each half to one of the other strips, end-to-end, so that you have two short strips and two long ones. Prepare each strip following the instructions on page 121.

10 Use a neutral-coloured sewing thread to bind the edges of the quilt, beginning with the long sides, following the instructions on page 122.

3 Following the arrangement we have used (✂ 3) lay the squares out in ten rows of eight. If you are working to your own design, make sure you spread patterns and plains evenly across the quilt; avoid having squares of the same colour close to each other and try to put contrasting fabrics next to each other where possible.

Lively Weekend

These projects are a little more time-consuming than those in the first section, with some requiring a wider range of skills.

Even though these projects are a little more demanding, they are still suitable for beginners. Each one can be completed in a weekend, provided you have obtained all the necessary materials and equipment in advance.

Pink & Lavender Cot Quilt

The finished size of the quilt is approximately 94cm (37in) square, which is fine for a crib or bassinette. On a standard cot, it also allows sufficient tuck-in for the 'feet-to-foot' position. For a quilt that fits the full length of a cot, you need to add another two or three rows of squares, for which you will need additional fabric and wadding. You can also scale the quilt up to fit a large cot or single bed.

This baby's cot quilt features terrific 50s-style novelty fabrics, set off with soft-coloured plains arranged in a 'four-square' pieced design. The bias-cut (across the weave) striped border combines the colours of the two plains and creates a strong yet subtle frame. If you wish to make a quilt in bolder colours, perhaps for a boy, there is a suggestion for an alternative colourway in maroon and turquoise.

✄ you will need

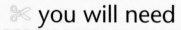

Fabric quantities assume a width of at least 115cm (45in)
Seam allowance 1cm (⅜in)

- 140cm (55in) dusty pink fabric

- 40cm (16in) lavender fabric

- 30cm (12in) each of two novelty fabrics (A) and (B)

- 20cm (8in) of a third novelty fabric (C)

- 70cm (28in) dusty pink-and-lavender striped fabric for the binding

- light-pink sewing thread

- 100cm (39in) square 55g (2oz) polyester wadding (batting)

- invisible quilting thread

- see also basic equipment (page 108)

- acetate for the templates, cut as follows:
  13cm (5⅛in) by 7.5cm (3in) rectangle
  13cm (5⅛in) square
  11cm (4⅜in) square

to make the quilt

1 Cut a 100cm (39in) square of fabric from the pink fabric for the back of the quilt and put to one side.

2 To make the checked squares, cut five 100 x 7.5cm (39 x 3in) strips from across the width of both the pink and the lavender fabrics. Sew the strips together lengthways in pairs, with a lavender strip to the left and a pink strip to the right, taking a 1cm (⅜in) seam (✂ 2). You should now have five pairs of strips. Press the seams open.

3 Using the rectangular template and tailor's chalk, carefully mark off every 7.5cm (3in) down each strip. You should have marked off 13 rectangles on each strip with a small piece left over at the end. Cut along the lines and discard the small pieces.

✂ **2**

cutting lines

discard

4 You will have 65 rectangles. You only need 64, so discard one. Place one rectangle in front of you, right side up, with the lavender square to the left. Place another rectangle on top of it, right side down, with the lavender square to the right. (Note that if your fabric has an obvious grain, you will need to make sure this runs from top to bottom when you assemble your squares.)

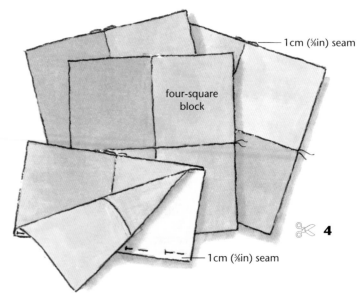

1cm (⅜in) seam

four-square block

✂ **4**

1cm (⅜in) seam

Pin the rectangles together along the bottom edge, with the pinheads to the left (✂ 4). Machine-sew together, taking a 1cm (⅜in) seam. Press the seam open. Continue in this way until you have 32 checked squares.

5 Using the 13cm (5⅛in) square template, cut twelve squares from each of fabrics (A) and (B), and eight squares from fabric (C). You may wish to 'fussy-cut' these squares ensuring each square contains an interesting part of the design. Once you have cut out the squares, centre the 11cm (4⅜in) square template on the wrong side of each of them and draw around it with tailor's chalk to give a seam allowance of 1cm (⅜in) all round.

6 Working with the fabrics right side uppermost, lay out each row of eight squares, alternating a checked square and a novelty fabric square. Each checked square should have a lavender square at the top left-hand corner.
 Row one: checked square, fabric (A), checked square, fabric (B), checked square, fabric (C), checked square, fabric (A).

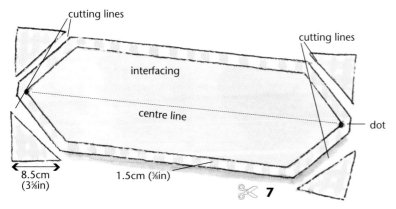

cutting lines

cutting lines

interfacing

centre line

dot

8.5cm (3⅜in)

1.5cm (⅝in)

✂ 7

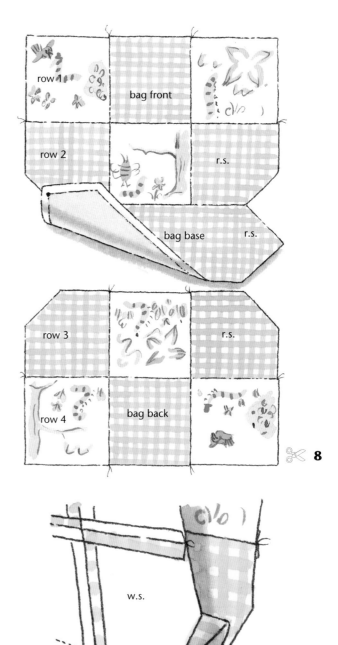

row 1

bag front

row 2

r.s.

bag base

r.s.

row 3

r.s.

row 4

bag back

✂ 8

w.s.

c/o

✂ 9

7 Take the base of the bag and an erasable marker and, on the wrong side of the fabric, mark a dot at each end on the centre line, 1.5cm (⅝in) in from the short edges. Use the triangle template (page 132) to mark and cut a triangle from each corner. Cut two pieces of interfacing 53 x 16cm (20¾ x 6¼in) and, again, trim a triangle from each corner using the template. Take one piece of interfacing (reserve the other for later) and centre it on the wrong side of the base of the bag. Iron in place following the manufacturer's instructions (✂ 7).

8 To assemble the bag, arrange the bag front, the base and the back as shown in ✂ 8. Ensure that rows three and four are upside down in relation to rows one and two. With right sides together, pin, then sew, the base – still using cream sewing thread – to the front and back along the bottom straight seam lines. Do not press the seams open.

9 Place the front of the bag against the back, right sides together. Fold the base in half and position between the front and back panels. Fold one half of the base up towards you and pin, then sew, a 1.5cm (⅝in) seam along the diagonal edges, from the marked dot to the lower edge of the base (✂ 9). Turn the bag over and repeat on the other side.

10 Sew the sides of the bag from the marked dot up to the top edges on either side. Press the seam open and turn the bag right sides out.

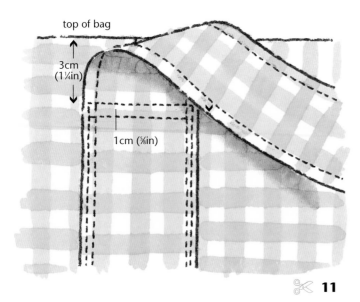

top of bag

3cm (1¼in)

1cm (⅜in)

✂ **11**

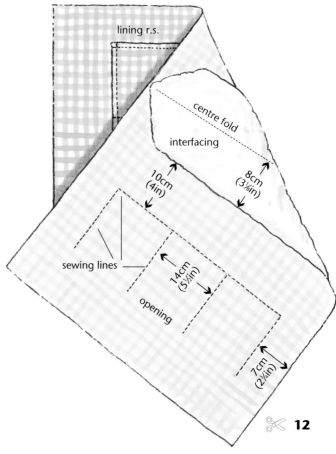

lining r.s.

centre fold

interfacing

10cm (4in)

8cm (3⅛in)

sewing lines

14cm (5½in)

opening

7cm (2¾in)

✂ **12**

11 Position the handle strips a third of the way across the bag on either side so they are centred over the vertical patchwork seams. The ends should butt up to each other on the base of the bag. Ensuring the straps are not twisted, pin them in place and, using primrose-yellow sewing thread, stitch between the top stitching and the edge of the strap, stopping 3cm (1⅜in) short of the top of the bag and sewing horizontally across the strap at this point. To strengthen, sew across the strap again 1.5cm (⅝in) lower (✂ 11).

12 Fold the lining fabric in half with short edges together. Measure 8cm (3⅛in) either side of the centre line and draw parallel lines to mark out the base of the lining. Centre the reserved interfacing on the wrong side of the base and iron in place (see ✂ 12). Cut the iron-on wadding to 88 x 53cm (34½ x 20¾in) and centre it on the wrong side of the lining, over the interfacing. Iron in place following the manufacturer's instructions.

13 Turn one long edge of each pocket piece down 1cm (⅜in) then another 1cm (⅜in). Pin then sew. Press 1.5cm (⅝in) turnings around the other three edges. Position the pocket pieces on either side of the base of the lining, with the bottom of each piece towards the centre (✂ 12). Sew in place using primrose-yellow sewing thread. Stitch each pocket piece at 14cm (5½in) intervals to form three pockets. Reinforce the points of strain at the top of each pocket by sewing several short stitches over one another and at right angles to the seam line.

4 Stitch-in-the-ditch along the seam lines using invisible quilting thread in the top of the machine and light-green in the bobbin (see page 112).

5 Cut five 7cm (2¾in) deep strips from the whole width of the giraffe print fabric. Cut one strip into two and join each half, end-to-end, to one of the other strips. Press the seams open. Prepare each strip following the instructions on page 121.

6 Using ochre sewing thread, bind the edges of the quilt beginning with the short ends, and following the instructions on page 122.

7 Using invisible thread in the top of your machine and light-green thread in the bobbin, stitch-in-the-ditch along the pinned binding seams following the instructions on page 112.

8 To make the pockets, fussy-cut four pandas and four giraffes (or similar) using template (C), and four lions and four elephants (or similar) using template (D). From the leafy parts of the leftover fabric (between the animals), cut eight pieces using template (A) and twelve pieces using template (b). Pin the pieces, right sides together to form four rows as follows (✂ 8):

    Row one: piece (A), lion, piece (B), giraffe, piece (B), elephant, piece (B), panda, piece (A)
    Row two: piece (A), panda, piece (B), lion, piece (B), giraffe, piece (B), elephant, piece (A)
    Row three: piece (A), elephant, piece (B), panda, piece (B), lion, piece (B), giraffe, piece (A)
    Row four: piece (A), giraffe, piece (B), elephant, piece (B), panda, piece (B), lion, piece (A)

Ensure the animal motifs are all the correct way up, then machine-sew using light-green sewing thread and press all seams open.

✂ **8**

9 Press the long top edge of each strip 1cm (⅜in) towards the wrong side, then press under again. Machine-sew in place using light-green sewing thread. Cut four 3.6cm (1⅜in) deep strips from across the width of the giraffe-print fabric. Pass through a tape-maker (see page 109), ironing the strips at the same time. (Trimming the end of each strip to a slight point will help the fabric through the tape maker.) If you have not got a bias-tape maker, press the strips in half lengthways, open out and press the raw edges to the centre. Do not open up the tape, but fold it in half lengthways along the top edge of the pockets (✂ 9). Pin and machine-sew through all layers using ochre sewing thread.

✂ **9**

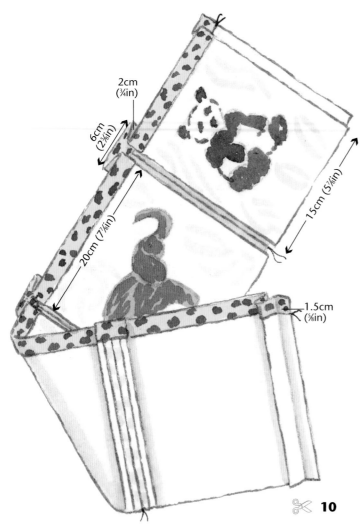

2cm
(¾in)

6cm
(2⅜in)

20cm (7⅞in)

15cm (5⅞in)

1.5cm
(⅝in)

✂ **10**

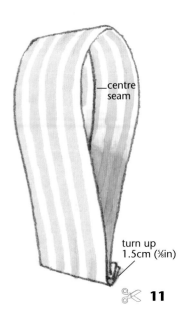

11 To make the loops for hanging, take the seven small strips of striped fabric and fold in half lengthways, wrong sides together and raw edges level. Pin along the raw edge and sew to form tubes. Press the seams open, then turn right sides out and press with the seam in the centre. Fold in half widthways with the seam on the inside and the raw ends level. Turn the raw ends under 1.5cm (⅝in), press, then stitch (✂ 11).

centre seam

turn up
1.5cm (⅝in)

✂ **11**

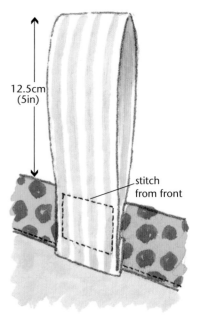

12 Working on the back of the quilt, position each loop along the top edge, centred above its corresponding colour section. The turning on the loop should face the back of the quilt and should lie across the binding seam line. (Ensure the loops are level at the top, otherwise they will not take the weight evenly on the hanging pole.) Machine-sew each strip in place by stitching a rectangle on the right side of the binding – that is from the front of the quilt (✂ 12).

12.5cm
(5in)

stitch from front

✂ **12**

10 Taking each row of pockets in turn, use the seam where one panel of fabric joins the next to press a series of box pleats along the length of the row (✂ 10). Form the end pleats by bringing the edge of the 6cm (2⅜in) section across to within 2cm (¾in) of the raw edge, and pressing. Then press the raw edges 1.5cm (⅝in) to the wrong side, so that a 5mm (³⁄₁₆in) strip projects beyond the pleat (✂ 10). Pin, then tack, all pleats in place, press under and tack 1.5cm (⅝in) along the bottom edge of each strip.

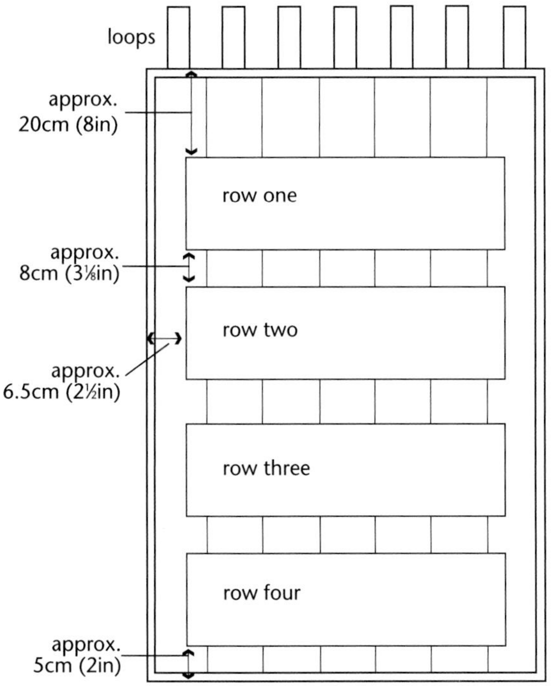
loops
approx. 20cm (8in)
row one
approx. 8cm (3⅛in)
row two
approx. 6.5cm (2½in)
row three
row four
approx. 5cm (2in)

✄ 13

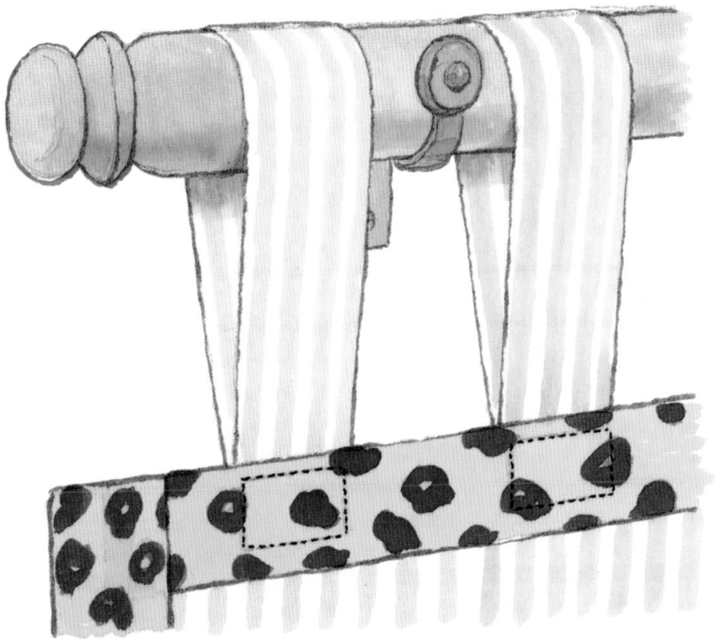

13 Position each row of pockets on the quilt and stitch in place (✄ 13). When sewing between the box pleats, ensure you do not catch the edges. When sewing close to the binding, lift the presser foot with the needle still in the fabric, and remove the pleat from under the presser foot, snipping any tacking if necessary, then tuck the pleat back underneath and continue sewing. Sew backwards and forwards twice at points of strain.

14 Decide on the position of the quilt on the wall (the top pockets must be easy for a child to reach without stretching). The curtain pole needs to be approximately 11cm (4⅜in) above your chosen position for the top edge of the quilt. Fix pole brackets firmly to the wall using appropriate fixings. Slot the loops onto the pole and hang the quilt.

Alternative

Instead of using fabric with widely spaced motifs, you can use an all-over jungle print to make the pockets for this wall hanging. It should measure 100 x 110cm (39 x 43in) and should be cut into four 106 x 23cm (41¾ x 9in) strips from across the width.

Take the first and third rows and measure from the left as follows, making a small mark in the top and bottom seam allowances, and taking the next measurement from that: 6cm (2⅜in), 20cm (7⅞in), 8cm (3⅛in), 15cm (5⅞in), 8cm (3⅛in), 20cm (7⅞in), 8cm (3⅛in), 15cm (5⅞in), 6cm (2⅜in). Reverse the order for the second and fourth rows, so: 6cm (2⅜in), 15cm (5⅞in), 8cm (3⅛in), 20cm (7⅞in), 8cm (3⅛in), 15cm (5⅞in), 8cm (3⅛in), 20cm (7⅞in), 6cm (2⅜in).

Draw a dot in the seam allowance to mark the centre line of each 8cm (3⅛in) section. Press these into box pleats by bringing the edges of the front pocket section across to the centre line (✄ 10). Follow steps 10 to 14 to complete the project.

Baby's Love Blanket

Ideal for use in a buggy (baby carriage) or with a car seat, this little quilt makes a perfect gift for a newborn. Because the blanket is so small, it doesn't require complex quilting – the three quilted hearts are sufficient if you use good-quality bonded wadding – and the fabrics used make a refreshing change from the usual baby colours. This quilt would also make a very smart topper for a doll's bed.

The finished size of the quilt is approximately 50 x 42cm (20 x 16½in). Alternatively you can scale it up to fit a large cot or single bed (see page 131), or use it as a wall hanging (see page 124).

✄ you will need

Fabric quantities assume a width of at least
   110cm (43in)
Seam allowance 1cm (⅜in)

- 50cm (20in) dark-pink fabric for the backing

- 20cm (8in) pink marbled fabric for binding

- 20cm (8in) lime-green fabric

- 20cm (8in) green-and-white small gingham
  check

- 20cm (8in) pink batik heart-motif fabric

- 10cm (4in) fusible webbing, 91cm (36in)
  wide

- dark-pink, shaded (space-dyed) machine-
  embroidery thread

- 56cm (22in) long by 46cm (18in) wide
  55g (2oz) polyester wadding (batting)

- light-green and dark-pink sewing threads

- one skein lime-green stranded embroidery
  thread

- one skein dark-pink stranded embroidery
  thread

- see also basic equipment (page 108)

- thin card or acetate for the templates,
  cut as follows:
  heart (see page 132)
  12cm (4¾in) square
  10cm (4in) square
  7cm (2¾in) square
  5cm (2in) square

61

to make the blanket

1 Cut a 56 x 46cm (22 x 18in) rectangle from dark-pink fabric for the backing, and set aside. Cut four 5cm (2in) wide binding strips from the pink marbled fabric, two 43cm (17in) long and two 56cm (22in) long.

2 Using the 12cm (4¾in) and 7cm (2¾in) square templates, cut the fabric as follows:
• lime-green fabric: three large squares and eight small ones
• dark-pink fabric: two large squares and six small ones
• pink marbled fabric: two large squares and five small ones
• green-and-white gingham fabric: three large squares and eight small ones
• batik heart-motif fabric: two large squares and five small ones

3 Iron a 9cm (3½in) square of fusible webbing to the back of the remnants of the dark-pink fabric, and a 9 x 18cm (3½ x 7in) rectangle to the back of the remnants of the pink marbled fabric. Using the heart template cut one heart from the dark-pink fabric and two from the pink marbled fabric. Centre the dark-pink heart on a large lime-green square and the pink marbled hearts on two green-and-white gingham squares. Iron in place, following the manufacturer's instructions. Use satin stitch to machine-sew around the hearts using pink-shaded machine-embroidery thread or, if you prefer, hand-embroider just inside the edge of each heart at step 10.

4 Lay out the large squares in rows as follows (✄ 4):
Row one: lime-green square, dark-pink square, gingham square
Row two: pink marbled square, gingham square, batik square
Row three: lime-green square, dark-pink square, lime-green square
Row four: batik square, gingham square, pink marbled square

5 Following the instructions on page 110, pin, then machine-sew, the three large squares in each row, using light-green sewing thread and taking a 1cm (⅜in) seam. For accuracy, use the 10cm (4in) square template to mark the seam lines. Press the seams open.

6 Join the small squares to form four border strips as follows, pinning a scrap of paper with the strip number on the left-hand square of each strip, see page 110. For accuracy, use the 5cm (2in) square template to mark the seam lines:
Strip one: pink marble, lime green, dark pink, gingham, batik, lime green, pink marble, gingham
Strip two: gingham, pink marble, lime green, batik, gingham, dark pink, lime green, batik
Strip three: gingham, batik, lime green, dark pink,

✄ **4**

✂ you will need

Fabric quantities assume a width of at least 110cm (43in) unless stated otherwise*
Seam allowance 1.5cm (⅝in)

- 210cm (83in) red fabric with widely spaced white dots for backing, binding and squares (*width at least 155cm (61in), or join two lengths of narrower fabric, see page 111)

- 30cm (12in) fine yellow-and-white check

- 30cm (12in) light-blue fabric with red dots

- 30cm (12in) white fabric with fine light-blue stripes

- 30cm (12in) green fabric with white dots

- 30cm (12in) yellow fabric

- 30cm (12in) light-blue fabric with white dots

- 30cm (12in) pink fabric with white dots

- 30cm (12in) yellow alphabet fabric

- 20cm (8in) red fabric with closely spaced white dots

- 20cm (8in) red fabric

- 30cm (12in) mid-blue fabric with fine blue dots

- 130cm (51in) blue alphabet fabric

- 130 x 46cm (51 x 18in) fusible webbing

- red, yellow, green, light blue, pink and mid-blue machine-embroidery threads

- neutral-coloured and red sewing threads

- 140 x 160cm (55 x 63in) 55g (2oz) polyester wadding (batting)

- invisible quilting thread

- see also basic equipment (page 108)

- thin card or acetate for the templates, cut as follows:
  21cm (8¼in) square
  18cm (7⅛in) square

to make the quilt

1 From the red fabric with widely spaced white dots, cut a piece 180cm (71in) long from the width of the fabric for the backing. Set to one side. You will be left with a strip 30cm (12in) deep. Using the 21cm (8¼in) square template, cut four squares from this strip and reserve the leftover piece of fabric for the letter 'U'.

2 Cut 21cm (8¼in) squares from the fabrics as follows (required number listed in brackets), reserving any leftovers for the letters):
• fine yellow-and-white check fabric (five)
• light-blue fabric with red dots (two)
• white fabric with fine light-blue stripes (four)
• green fabric with white dots (three)
• yellow fabric (two)
• light-blue fabric with white dots (three)
• pink fabric with white dots (three)
• yellow alphabet fabric (four)

3 Make your patterns for the letters, either by enlarging the templates on pages 139–141 or by printing out your own 475pt letters on a computer. (Set the computer to print on the 'outline' setting to save ink.) Use the printed or enlarged letters as your patterns.

4 Cut the fusible webbing into 15cm (6in) squares – one for each letter. Iron the webbing onto the back of the fabrics as follows:
• red fabric with closely spaced white dots: letters A and R
• yellow fabric: letters B, I, M and Z
• green fabric with white dots: letters C, J and Y
• pink fabric with white dots: letters D and P
• white fabric with fine light-blue stripes: letters E and Q
• light-blue fabric with white dots: letters F, O and V
• red fabric: letters G, K, S and X
• mid-blue fabric with fine blue dots: letters H, L, N, T and W
• red fabric with widely spaced white dots: letter U

5 Using the patterns, cut out each letter and centre on its appropriate square. Bond in place following the manufacturer's instructions. If you wish, machine-sew satin stitch around each letter using a matching colour of machine-embroidery thread.

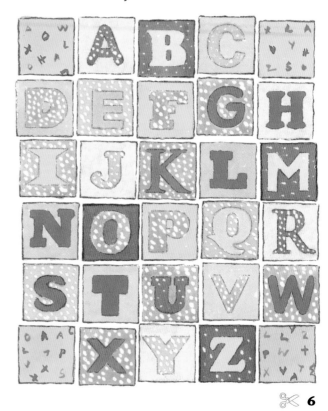

✂ **6**

6 Arrange the squares in rows (✂ 6), and pin in each row together following the instructions on page 110. For accuracy, mark the seam allowance on the back of each square using the 18cm (7⅛in) square template and a vanishing marker. Machine-stitch the squares together using a neutral-coloured thread, and press the seams open.

7 Join the rows together, ensuring the seams align (see page 111). Press the seams open.

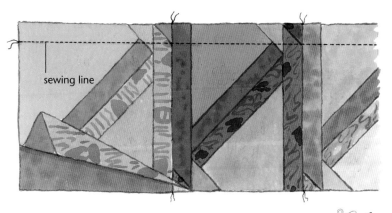

sewing line

✂ 6

6 Join the rows together in the same way, ensuring they are in the correct order. As you sew, make sure you stitch across each seam where the point of the small triangle in the seam allowance meets the vertical seam (✂ 6). Press the seams open.

7 Use the quilt top as a template to cut the backing fabric 3cm (1⅛in) bigger all round. Cut a piece of wadding to the same size as the backing fabric. Lay the backing fabric on the floor wrong side up (if applicable), lay the wadding on top, then centre the quilt top on that. There should be an even border of wadding showing all round. Pin-baste the whole quilt, avoiding the seams, and following the instructions on page 112.

8 Using invisible quilting thread in the top of your machine and a neutral-coloured thread in the bobbin, quilt along all seam lines by stitching-in-the-ditch (see page 112).

9 Cut five binding strips 11cm (4⅜in) deep from the width of the binding fabric. Cut one binding strip into two equal lengths and sew each piece, end-to-end, onto another binding strip. Press the seams open. You now have two shorter and two longer pieces.

10 Prepare the binding strips following the instructions on page 121.

11 Using a neutral-coloured thread, and following the instructions on page 122, bind the quilt, starting with the longer sides.

Alternatives
Choose other novelty fabrics, or use just one printed and one plain fabric to make the sawtooth squares.

Night-time Cushion

The smiling moon on this large, crazy patchwork cushion is friendly and sleepy, making it perfect for a child's bedroom. Although it may appear complicated, crazy patchwork is actually very simple to do. The joins are over sewn with fancy embroidery, which helps to strengthen them and softens the transition between fabrics. If you don't have a sewing machine that can do embroidery, you can either use machine zigzag or hand-embroider the stitches.

The finished size of the cushion is approximately 65cm (25½in) square. You can also convert the front panel into a wall hanging.

✂ you will need

Fabric quantities assume a width of at least 110cm (43in)
Seam allowance 1.5cm (⅝in)

- 60cm (24in) black fabric with stars and moons for patchwork and binding

- assortment of fat quarters and offcuts of about ten star and moon fabrics with black, navy and blue backgrounds

- 15 x 10cm (6 x 4in) offcut of light-grey crackle-effect fabric for moon

- 70cm (28in) navy-and-gold flecked fabric for the cushion back

- 15 x 10cm (6 x 4in) fusible webbing

- blue sewing thread

- off-white and yellow shaded machine-embroidery threads

(or stranded embroidery threads for hand-embroidery)

- mid-grey and bright-red stranded embroidery threads

- 65cm (25½in) square cushion pad or pillow

- 55cm (21½in) lightweight navy zip

- approx. 300cm (118in) no. 4 cotton piping cord

- see also basic equipment (page 108)

- thin paper for the pattern, cut as follows: 68cm (26¾in) square

- thin paper for the templates (pages 134–135)

Note This cushion must not be used as a pillow for sleeping on, nor given to babies under one year old.

to make the cushion cover

1 From the fabric you have chosen for the binding, make 5cm (2in) wide bias strips following the instructions on page 121. Join where necessary with blue sewing thread to form a 280cm (110in) continuous strip. Set to one side and use the remnants of the fabric for the crazy patchwork.

2 Trace the templates onto the thin paper. Using one of the plainer, darker fabrics with a small-scale design (to give a good contrast with the moon motif) cut the six-sided central shape. Reverse the moon motif and trace onto the paper backing of the fusible webbing. Iron onto the wrong side of the grey crackle print, following the webbing manufacturer's instructions.

3 Cut out the motif using small, sharp scissors. Peel off the backing paper and iron the motif in the correct position on the central shape. Machine-stitch around the edge of the moon using off-white machine thread and satin stitch, then backstitch the eye in grey stranded embroidery thread and the mouth in bright red.

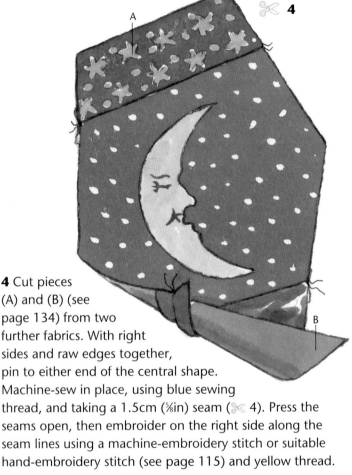

4 Cut pieces (A) and (B) (see page 134) from two further fabrics. With right sides and raw edges together, pin to either end of the central shape. Machine-sew in place, using blue sewing thread, and taking a 1.5cm (⅝in) seam (✂ 4). Press the seams open, then embroider on the right side along the seam lines using a machine-embroidery stitch or suitable hand-embroidery stitch (see page 115) and yellow thread.

2 Cut all the 16.5cm (6½in) squares in half diagonally using a rotary cutter (see page 109) and place in three piles, one for each fabric design.

3 Centre the 17cm (6¾in) square template on the wrong side of each 20cm (7⅞in) fabric square and draw round it with erasable pen to mark the seam allowance. The seam allowance should be of equal width on all sides of the square, and should measure 1.5cm (⅝in) wide.

4 Create four piles of shapes:
   Pile one: pink paisley fabric and blue-and-red spotted fabric
   Pile two: blue floral fabric and green, white and red check fabric
   Pile three: white floral fabric and blue, red and pink check fabric
   Pile four: blue paisley fabric and pink-and-red spotted fabric

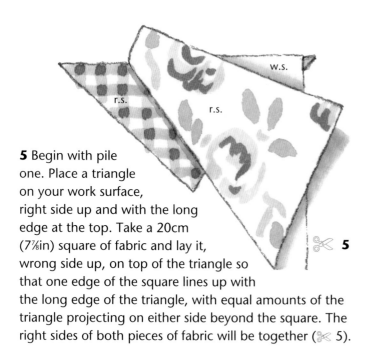

5 Begin with pile one. Place a triangle on your work surface, right side up and with the long edge at the top. Take a 20cm (7⅞in) square of fabric and lay it, wrong side up, on top of the triangle so that one edge of the square lines up with the long edge of the triangle, with equal amounts of the triangle projecting on either side beyond the square. The right sides of both pieces of fabric will be together (✂ 5).

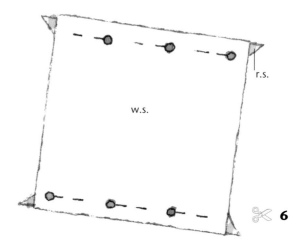

6 Pin along the seam line so the sharp ends of the pins point to the left. Turn the square right round through 180 degrees. Take a second triangle and repeat step 5 (✂ 6). Do this with all the squares in each pile.

7 Take each square in turn and, using a neutral-coloured sewing thread, machine-sew along one seam, with the pins on the top surface of the fabric and the bulk of the fabric to your left. The pins should have their heads towards you for easy removal as you sew along the marked seam line. Without cutting the thread (known as 'chaining', see page 111), take another square and sew this in the same way, leaving a gap of between 1–2cms (½–1in) between the pieces. Continue like this until you have sewn each square in the pile along one seam.

8 Cut the thread between the squares and stack them back in their piles. Starting again, take each square in turn and machine-sew the second seam. Complete each pile of squares before you start the next, until you have sewn both seams on all squares.

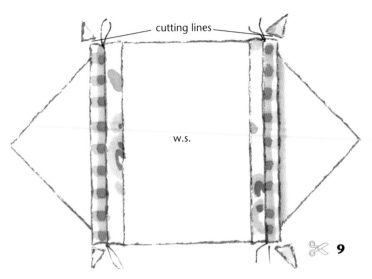

cutting lines

w.s.

✂ **9**

9 Press the seams open on each square and snip the four projecting points level (✂ 9). Do this to all the squares in each pile.

10 Take a square from pile one, now with two attached triangles, and position it on your work surface wrong side up. Turn the square so the triangles are to the left and right. Repeat steps 5 to 9 with two new triangles each time, until you have sewn all the squares.

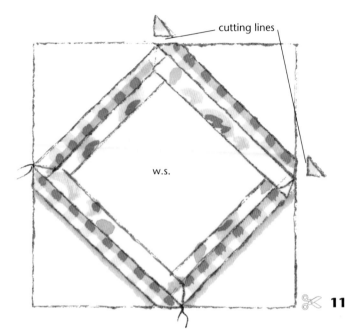

cutting lines

w.s.

✂ **11**

11 Press the seams open on each square and snip off the projecting points level with the edge of the larger square you have created (✂ 11).

12 Place the 24cm (9⁷⁄₁₆in) square template on the wrong side of each large square and repeat the instructions in step 3.

13 Take three squares from pile one (1) and two squares from pile two (2). Arrange them on your work surface in a row in the order 1-2-1-2-1, then pin them together, wrong sides facing, to form a strip. Repeat three more times until you have used up all the squares in piles one and two. Sew the seams and press all the seams open.

14 Take three squares from pile three (3) and two squares from pile four (4). Pin them together, following the same instructions as for step 13, except the order will now be 3-4-3-4-3. Repeat this whole step twice more until you have used up all the squares in piles three and four. Machine-sew along each pinned seam, and press the seams open.

know what colour thread to use. Unless there is a predominant fabric colour, choose a neutral colour such as dark beige or medium grey. If the fabrics tend to be in dark colours, use a dark grey, navy or black. Always make sure the tension is correct in your machine to avoid stitches showing between patches, which can look unsightly if the thread isn't a good match.

For tacking (basting) use a contrast colour. Avoid using dark thread on light fabric however, because it may leave fibres behind on removal, making the fabric look dirty. Be sure to use colourfast thread, too, so that the colour does not transfer to your fabric. Don't be tempted to use cheap thread, either: tacking thread is stronger than normal sewing thread and is less likely to break.

Quilting thread is much stronger than usual sewing thread, and is often wax coated to make it slightly stiffer. This means it is not ideal for machine-quilting as it can stick, but is perfect for quilting by hand.

Invisible quilting thread, which comes in clear and smoke, is good for quilting multicoloured projects because it doesn't show up. It is also known as nylon monofilament thread and invisible nylon thread. Invisible quilting thread may melt if you use a very hot iron on it.

Machine-embroidery thread, which is thicker than standard thread, can be used for quilting if you wish the stitches to be prominent.

Wadding (batting)

Wadding is the soft padding that usually makes up the middle part of the quilt 'sandwich' (see page 111). Even in these days of metrication, wadding still tends to be sold in ounces.

Polyester is the most popular wadding material, and 70g (2oz) is the most suitable weight. Heavier weights are available, but anything thicker than 135g (4oz) can be very difficult to work with. The most usual colour for polyester wadding is white, but it is also available in black for use with dark fabrics so any 'bearding' will not show.

Always buy the best-quality wadding you can afford. Some polyester varieties compact irrevocably when ironed – these tend to have a slightly crispy feel to them. Soft, silky wadding is more resilient and drapes better when an item is finished. Opt for bonded waddings where possible. Here, the fibres are treated with resin or glue to prevent them shifting about inside the quilt once it is made and you are unlikely to have problems with bearding. The resin does not affect the drape or handle of the wadding.

Cotton wadding is the main alternative to polyester. It gives quite a different feel and lends more of an 'antique' look to a project. Cotton-wadded quilts look much flatter, but they are heavier and warmer, which may make them too warm for a child's bed. In the past, cotton-wadded quilts required very close quilting to hold the wadding in place, as it tended to pull apart with use. This is why antique quilts are often very densely quilted. Modern needled-cotton waddings are a great improvement, however. They are more stable and the fibres are less likely to pull apart.

Cotton wadding is more costly than polyester, but comes in very wide widths, which is great for making larger quilts. Cotton wadding is also a good option for wall hangings, where you want the quilt to hang flat. Manufacturers may recommend that you wash cotton wadding carefully before making up a project and you will need to follow such recommendations carefully.

Wadding can be bought from a roll or in pre-cut packs of standard sizes. In some instances the wadding will come with instructions as to how closely a project should be quilted and how to wash it. Sample packs of wadding are available so you can try out different options. Iron-on wadding does not need quilting into place. It is fairly thin and most useful for wadding smaller parts of a project, rather than an entire quilt.

Equipment

Quilting can be carried out with the minimum of equipment and if you sew regularly you will probably have most items already. There are certain tools and gadgets that are popular with quilters, which will allow you to work faster and more accurately. As your interest in patchwork grows, it is a good idea to look out for specialist patchwork and quilting shops and fairs, where you can pick up the more unusual products.

Basic kit

There are a number of tools that are standard in a quilter's basic equipment.

Pencil

Scissors

Safety pins

Tape measure

Calculator

Ruler

Iron

Thimble

Pins and pincushion
Long pins are best for quilting – at least 2.5cm (1in).

Needles
Machine-sewing: universal needle sizes 70 and 80 are suitable for quilting. Hand-sewing: short needles, called 'betweens' are used for hand-quilting.

Sewing machine
At the most basic level, you can use a machine that does just straight stitches, while a swing-needle machine, which does zigzag stitches, is useful for projects requiring appliqué work. There are some dedicated quilting machines on the market, as well as some that are capable of a wide range of embroidery stitches.

Erasable fabric marker pens
Erasable markers make easy work of transferring designs and motifs onto fabric (see page 119). There are two types: vanishing and water-soluble.

With either type of erasable marker, it is very important not to iron over the marks before attempting to remove them: this can set them and render them permanent. Having erased water-soluble marker lines, it is also important to allow the fabric to dry completely before pressing or ironing, otherwise the lines may reappear and, again, become difficult or impossible to remove.

Tailor's chalk
The easiest way to use chalk is in the form of a dressmaker's chalk pencil.

Chalk is particularly useful for dark fabrics, which can otherwise be difficult to mark effectively, and you can usually remove it simply by brushing it off or wiping it over with a damp cloth. Chalk lines are not usually clear enough to be used for transferring embroidery motifs to fabric.

Quilting clips

These are round metal clips that are used for keeping a quilt rolled up and out of the way while you are machining a particular part of it (bicycle clips can be used instead).

Optional extras

In addition to your basic kit there are other pieces of equipment that can make life easier and speed up some of the quilt-making processes.

Rotary cutter

This gadget allows you to cut several layers of fabric at once and increases accuracy at the same time. They must always be used with a self-healing cutting mat, pushing the gadget away from you through the fabric, rather than pulling it towards you.

Self-healing cutting mat

These come in two thicknesses. The thinner mats are suitable for use with rotary cutters only, while the thicker ones can also be used with craft knives. Rest on a hard, even surface when cutting and keep flat and away from radiators, heaters and direct sunlight when not in use to prevent distortion and buckling.

Squared paper

A pad of paper with 5mm (3⁄16in) faint squares is ideal for planning designs and working out fabric quantities. You can draw your designs to scale, using a number of squares to represent 10cm (4in).

Basting spray

This is an aerosol glue that can be used to hold the layers of a quilt together for stitching without the need for pinning and basting. The glue is simply sprayed onto the wrong side of both the backing fabric and the quilt top and, once the glue is tacky, the surfaces are pressed together. The adhesion lessens over time, and the glue washes out when you launder the quilt. Sometimes it has a strong chemical smell, which really makes it unsuitable for use on quilts for babies.

'O' weights

These circular plastic weights have small spikes in the bottom that grip fabric when you stand them on it. They are very useful for holding fabric flat on the floor or keeping it steady on the table while you cut it.

Tape-maker

This is a metal, funnel-shaped gadget used for converting a strip of fabric into professional-looking binding. They come in different widths and are not adjustable, so you need a different size for each width of binding.

Seam ripper or unpicker

This is an essential tool for quick unpicking of machine stitching. Use the tool with care to avoid tearing the fabric with its sharp point.

Embroidery hoop

This is a metal and plastic or wooden hoop over which you stretch fabric when embroidering it to prevent the fabric puckering.

Seam gauge

This is a small, adjustable gadget for setting a specific measurement – useful for making turnings.

Light box

If you intend to do much sewing a light box would be a very useful acquisition. It is ideal for tracing through light-coloured fabric for embroidery and for reversing a design for appliqué by tracing over the back of a photocopy. You can buy small light boxes quite cheaply. Taping your work to a sunny window works almost as well, but isn't quite so comfortable to work at.

Patchwork & Quilting Techniques

Almost all of the projects share similar patchwork and quilting techniques. Once you have built up a little skill, the steps will start to become second nature to you.

Patchwork

Also known as piecing, patchwork involves stitching small, geometrical patches of patterned fabrics together to form a larger design. Accuracy is vital, since a small discrepancy can result in a big error across the width of a quilt. This means any templates and cutting out must be precise, as must your sewing.

Joining patches

Patches have very narrow seam allowances, which can be fiddly to sew. For greater flexibility and to make the sewing easier a wider allowance of 1cm (⅜in) or 1.5cm (⅝in) is used for most of the projects in this book.

1 Sewing accurately along the seam lines is very important, so mark them on the back of each shape using a second, smaller template. Centre the smaller template on the back of each fabric shape and draw around it.

2 Lay the patches out, right side up, in the order you wish them to appear. In many projects, the patches in the horizontal rows are joined first and then the rows are joined from top to bottom to form the quilt panel.

3 When you come to join the rows together, mark the row number in the seam allowance of each left-most square. This way you will also know which is the left-hand end of each row.

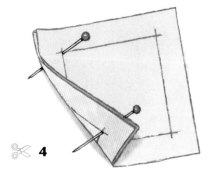

✂ **4**

4 Pin the shapes together in the correct order, right sides together. You can check that the seams line up with each other by pushing a pin through before you attach each square to its neighbour (✂ 4).

5 Machine-sew along all the seams, with the pins on the top surface of the fabric and the bulk of the fabric to your left. The pins should have their heads towards you for easy removal (✂ 5). Sew along the marked seam lines and take the pins out as you sew. Don't sew over pins as this can break the needle. Press all the seams open.

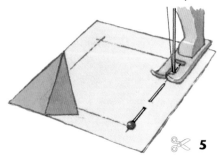

✂ **5**

the teeth. Pivot again at the next corner, then sew up the other long side of the zip, pivot again, and come back to your starting point across the top of the zip. Clip the threads, pull through to the wrong side of the fabric and tie off. Remove the tacking and open the zip.

6 Take the bias binding and fold it around the piping cord. Ensure the cord is straight, but do not stretch it. Pin along the length of the binding, close to the cord. Machine-sew along the length of the binding, about 5mm from the cord, using a zipper foot.

7 Lay out the cushion back, right side up, with the zip running from top to bottom. Pin the covered piping around the edge, raw edges level, so that the two ends of the piping meet at the centre of the bottom edge of the cushion cover. Snip the bias binding up to the machine-stitching to allow the piping to lie flat around the corners (✂ 7).

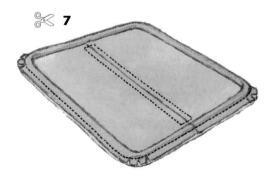

8 Sew the ends of the cord together, trimming them if necessary, so they remain butted up, but don't overlap them. Trim the binding so one end overlaps the other by about 2cm (¾in). Fold one end under by 1cm (⅜in) and wrap it over the other. Tack the binding in place along the seam line (✂ 8).

9 Lay the cushion front, wrong side up, on to the back, checking that any motifs are the correct way up and the zip is open. Ensure all the raw edges

✂ **8**

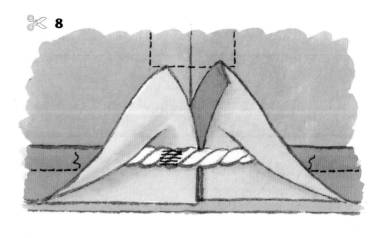

are level, then pin, tack and machine around the seam line. Remove any visible tacking, then turn the cover right side out through the open zip. Press the cover carefully, avoiding the zip teeth if it is nylon. Insert the cushion pad and close the zip.

Customizing & Making Variations

You can make up the projects in this book by following the instructions exactly. But you may wish to branch out and make up a quilt that is a variation on one of the designs. Here is advice on how to do this.

Creating a different colourway

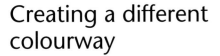

Always try out colour combinations before you buy your fabric and start to make up the quilt. Obtain small samples of fabric (you can often buy packs of postage-stamp-sized swatches from patchwork mail order companies), or buy the minimum quantities of the fabrics you are considering (usually 20cm or 25cm (6in or 9¾in) off the roll, or buy a ready-cut fat eighth).

Try the colours against each other, in the same ratios as they appear on the quilt. For example, if only a small amount of a colour appears on a quilt, your alternative colour should be represented only by a tiny piece in your samples. Take time to consider the combinations, and don't be afraid to try other colours.

One way of finding interesting colour combinations is simply to group fabrics randomly. If you have built an interesting stash or collection of fabrics, you can try taking out selections of fabrics at random and seeing how they look together. While this book is not intended to explain how to design your own quilts from scratch, this is a very good way to get inspiration should you ever wish to create your own designs.

When used together, patterned fabrics look best if they have something in common with each other, for example similar colours, patterns or scale. Although antique quilts may feature a jumble of all types of fabrics and still look good, this can be because the fabrics were printed using a narrow range of vegetable or early synthetic dyes. These fade, which adds to the harmonious effect.

Today's fabrics, with their wide spectrum of colours, can look mesy if indiscriminately juxtaposed. The most successful way to work with a colourful patterned fabric is to use it as the starting point for your colour scheme and match simpler patterns and plains to it.

Changing motifs

If you or your child has a preference for certain motifs, and these don't appear on the project, you can, of course, substitute or add them to the design. The Wild West Quilt on page 78, for example, is emblazoned with stars, but if you prefer, you could change these to hearts, or use a variety of simple motifs, such as hearts, stars, diamonds, circles, triangles, letters of the alphabet and so on. You can also add motifs or names to quilts.

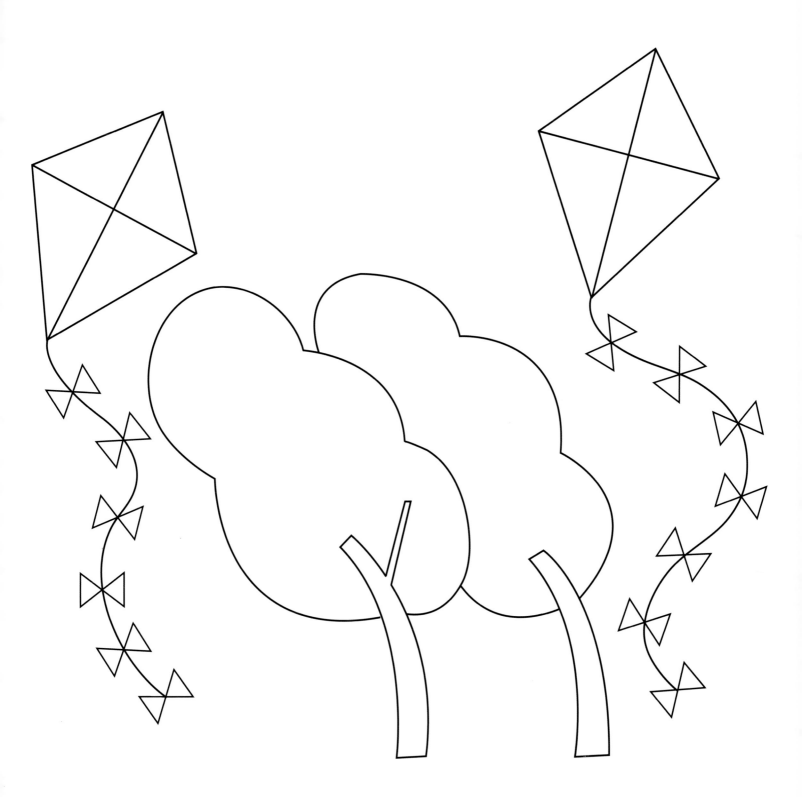

Alphabet Quilt

Sunny Sawtooth Quilt (100%)

Wild West Quilt

Acknowledgements

Author's acknowledgements

First, I would like to say a big thank you to my husband Kevin for being so enthusiastic about my quilts, for offering helpful criticism, and for putting up with months of chaos, upheaval and clutter in the house without complaint while I was working on this project. Equally, I would like to say a huge thank you to my daughter Isabelle for inspiring me with her unceasing creativity and enthusiasm, for being patient while I was working on this book, and for her beautiful drawings, some of which feature in these quilts.

Next, there are several companies to whom I am indebted for their assistance. I would like to extend very grateful thanks to Julie Gill at Coats Crafts UK for her unstinting helpfulness and generosity in supplying Coats and Prym quilting equipment and Anchor embroidery cottons. Thank you too to Vilene for their generosity in supplying all the wadding for the quilts in this book. I would also like to thank Zoffany for supplying fabrics from their delightful Caboodle Range, which are used in the projects on pages 10, 44, 54 and 78. Thanks too to Rowan for supplying fabrics from the inspirational Kaffe Fassett range; these are used in the projects on pages 14, 40, 50, 64 and 82. Thank you too to Zoe Phayre-Mudge of ZPM for supplying the fantastic novelty fabrics used in the project on page 40 and its alternative colourway.

Finally, I would like to thank the team at Hamlyn for being such fun to work with and their enthusiasm for this project. In particular I would like to thank Doreen Palamartschuck-Gillon who commissioned me, Sarah Tomley and Jessica Cowie who managed the project, and Anne Southgate who edited the text.

Publisher's acknowledgements

The publisher would like to thank following for the supply of items for photography
Cheeky Monkeys for many wonderful toys.
www.cheekymonkeys.com
Damask for the Home for bedding, towels and children's night clothes. 3–4 Beoxholme House, New Kings Road, SW6 4AA
Tel 020 7731 3553 www.damask.co.uk
Ecos Paints for superb environmentally friendly paints. Unit 34 Heysham Business Park, Middleton Road, Lancashire, LA3 3PP
Tel 01524 852371 www.ecospaints.com
The Holding Company for a variety of boxes and baskets. Tel 020 8445 2888
www.theholdingcompany.co.uk
The Pier for cushions, rugs and furniture.
Tel 0845 6091234 www.pier.co.uk
The White Company for bedding, towels, soft toys and childrens night cloths.
Tel 087099555 www.thewhiteco.com

Photography **Octopus Publishing Group Limited**/Graham Atkins-Hughes 1, 2, 4-5, 6, 8, 14, 15, 16, 17, 18, 19, 21, 22, 23, 24, 27, 28, 29, 30, 33, 34, 35, 36, 38, 40, 41, 43, 44, 45, 49, 50, 51, 54, 55, 56, 60, 61, 64, 65, 66, 68, 69, 70, 72, 74, 75, 82, 83, 85, 86, 87, 89, 90, 91, 92, 100, 101, 103, 108, 110, 114, 120, 124, 125, 126, 128, 129, 130, 131/Dominic Blackmore 10, 11, 13, 78, 79, 94, 95, 98, 104, 106, 119, 123, 127

Executive Editor Sarah Tomley
Editor Jessica Cowie
Executive Art Editor Joanna MacGregor
Design Jane Forster
Illustration Kate Simunek
Production Controller Manjit Sihra

Stockist and Suppliers

UK

Coats Crafts UK
PO Box 22
Lingfield House
Lingfield Point
McMullen Road
Darlington
DL1 1YQ
Tel 01325 394237
www.coatscrafts.co.uk
Distributors of sewing and embroidery threads, and patch-work and quilting equipment, including rotary cutters, rulers and cutting boards.

Rowan
Green Lane Mill
Holmfirth
West Yorkshire
HD7 1RW
Tel 01484 681881
www.knitrowan.com
Distributors of Kaffe Fassett patchwork and quilting fabrics.

Stitch-in-Time
293 Sandycombe Rd
Kew, TW9
Tel 020 8948 8462
www.stitchintimeuk.com
Fabric and equipment shop.

Strawberry Fayre
Chagford
Devon
TQ13 8EN
Tel 01647 433250
www.strawberryfayre.co.uk
Quilting fabrics and supplies by mail order.

Vilene
Freudenberg Nonwovens LP
Lowfield Business Park
Elland
West Yorkshire
HX5 5DX
Tel 01422 327900
www.vilene.com
Manufacturers of wadding and non-woven interlinings.

Zoffany
Talbot House
17 Church Street
Rickmansworth
Hertfordshire
WD3 1DE
Tel 08708 300 350
www.zoffany.com
Manufacturers of furnishing fabrics.

Contents

With many thanks, Connie, from *Sten og Stoffer* (Stones and Fabrics), for the beautiful fabrics, Thermolam and silk thread.

A big 'thank you' also to Pernille for opening your home once more for the photography.

Foreword

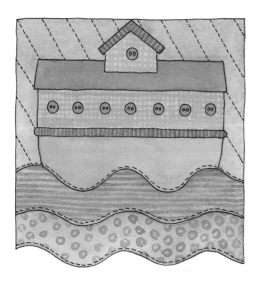

Unlike my previous books, this book has a recurring theme, being inspired by the tale of Noah's Ark from the Old Testament.

Some years ago in the Shaker shop in London, I saw a wonderful Ark made of wood. This idea got stored away and has now become a flock of happy, friendly animals. Some are just cuddy toys, while others have various practical functions, such as the coaster and placemat (page 42) or the fish bags (page 75).

For the smallest models in the book, such as the animals on page 31, you can easily make use of fabric oddments left over from larger projects. These little animals go very well with the cushion on page 38, which is shaped like Noah's Ark and features a pocket to hold your favourite animals. This would make a wonderful soft toy for a child – or anyone with a soft spot for the naïve. On the last pages of the book, there are various nice things to take with you when you go out – whether it is on a boating trip, a picnic, just to lounge in the garden or sit on the balcony. The colours of the designs are inspired by the light, the heat and the expectation of a beautiful summer day, but if you choose warmer tones, the picnic blanket, the seat cushion and the linings for the various baskets will provide a cosy feeling indoors as well. Almost symbolically, it has been raining continuously while I have been putting the finishing touches to Noah's Ark. So it has been perfect weather for immersing myself in the project. I hope that you too – whatever the weather – find the time to embark on the designs in this book.

With best wishes from Anne-Pia, September 2004

Materials and Equipment

This section briefly describes the materials and equipment used for the models in this book.

Scissors and cutting set

You will need a good pair of fabric scissors and, for cutting straight edges accurately, you will find a cutting set consisting of a rotary cutter, a ruler and a cutting board very helpful. The set can be purchased in hobby, quilting and sewing-accessories shops.

Pencil

For drawing on light fabrics, an ordinary 1B–3B sketching pencil can be used, and for dark fabrics, fabric chalks in a light shade. The marks from these will disappear over time.

Needle and thread

For machine sewing, you will need a size 70 or 80 needle. Stitch length for sewing should be set at 2.5–3.5, and for decorative stitching or topstitching, use a stitch length of 4.0.

It is always a good idea to test your stitching on a small piece of the chosen fabric, so you can adjust the stitch length and thread colour to suit the fabric, especially if you are working with several layers at once. For joining openings and for assembling, a size 9 or 10 sewing needle can be used, and for sewing on arms/legs or stitching through several/thick layers, use a large needle and strong thread.

It is a matter of taste whether cotton thread or synthetic thread is used, but it must match the fabric colour. For quilting and topstitching, quilting thread – cotton or silk – can be used, or 2-3-ply DMC embroidery thread, if preferred.

Fabrics

The models shown have been made in various types of cotton fabric. Where two fabrics are sewn together, they should have the same weight and weave.

If a model is likely to require machine washing now and then, it is a good idea to pre-wash the fabrics before joining the pieces. This will prevent colour runs and uneven shrinkage in the finished model.

Fabrics that do not match or coordinate can be dyed in a same dye bath. This will provide a matching 'base colour'. When dyeing, follow the instructions on the packet.

Towelling, which is used for the sheep cushion (page 46) and hot-water bottle cover (page 58), for example, can be purchased by the metre (yard), but it is also possible to cut the pattern pieces from towels.

Acrylic fleece, used for clothing, is also utilised in the book on the back of the picnic blanket (see page 103).

Stuffing

Synthetic fibrefill is used to stuff the various animals and cushion pads. This is available from toy-making suppliers.

Wadding

Wadding is available in sew-in or fusible (iron-on) versions. Both are suitable, but fusible wadding has the advantage that it can be attached to the fabric easily and it can be ironed on to the fabric before sewing and stuffing with fibrefill. It gives a nice, smooth surface to the finished product. Use a lightweight wadding approximately 2mm (⅛in) thick.

Interfacing

Interfacing is available in several qualities. In this book, it is used to support linen or very thin fabric, where the model has to be stuffed with fibrefill. Choose a soft to medium quality.

Insulated wadding

Insulated wadding is available in various qualities. Thermolam by Vilene is a good example and does not alter with use.

Pellets

Pellets are small plastic balls used to stuff toys. In this book, they are used to give models weight and stability when they are required to sit or stand.

Buttons

Buttons are sometimes used for practical purposes – for buttoning two sections together, for example – and sometimes they are purely decorative. The buttons should be sewn securely so that small children cannot pull them off.

Marking needle

A marking needle has become an indispensable tool for me. It is used when you have to mark up a fold, when you have to make a fold back, and on outside openings. A marking needle is simply a thick darning needle. You can glue a large pearl to it as a 'handle'.

Turning and stuffing stick

A turning and stuffing stick is simply a wooden stick that is sharpened with a pencil sharpener, but is not so sharp that it makes a hole in the fabric. It is a good idea to have sticks in different thicknesses – thin sticks are useful for very small things. As the name suggests, the stick is used for turning the fabric right side out and then for stuffing fibrefill into the model.

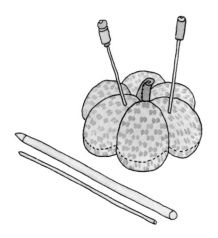

Techniques

Templates

When patterns need to be drawn on to the fabric, it is much easier if you have a template made from something a little stiffer and heavier than paper. The patterns can be transferred to template plastic and cut out, or they can be transferred to paper and glued on to cardboard, such as the back of a writing pad.

Centre front and centre back

The abbreviations 'CF' and 'CB' appear on some pattern pieces. They stand for centre front and centre back respectively.

Cutting measurements

As a general rule, all patterns and measurements include seam allowances, equivalent to a presser foot's seam allowance – approximately 7.5mm (a generous ¼in). There are, however, a few exceptions: when a pattern should be divided along a dividing line, the seam allowance should be added to that edge.

A presser foot's seam allowance

To sew with a presser foot's seam allowance means simply to guide the fabric under the presser foot so the raw edge is just visible to the right of the presser foot and the needle is placed in the centre position (see the illustration below right).

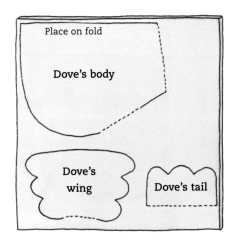

Place on fold

Dove's body

Dove's wing

Dove's tail

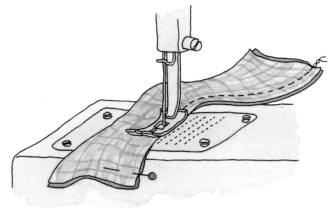

Sewing Techniques

Wrong-side sewing

The wrong-side sewing method (when pieces are sewn from the wrong side, with right sides facing) is used for many of this book's models. The simplicity of it is that the sewing is done before the fabric is cut. When two different pieces of fabric are used for hands/sleeves or feet/legs, the fabrics are sewn right sides together and the seam allowance is topstitched in place. Afterwards, the fabric is folded, the pattern drawn on top and then the pieces are sewn as described below before being cut out.

With very small items, such as pig snouts and the beaks of hens or geese, it can be difficult to close an opening neatly. On these small items, it is a good idea to cut a small slit in the back, which is then used for turning and filling. The slit should be joined together afterwards using overcast stitches.

1 Fold each fabric piece with right sides together and draw around the template, marking the opening for turning.

2 Sew along the drawn line, leaving the opening for turning as well as any other required openings such as those for the ears (see figure 1).

3 Cut out, allowing a narrow seam allowance of about 3mm (⅛in), except by the opening(s) where the allowance should be 5mm (¼in), as shown in figure 2.

4 Cut small notches in the seam allowances at inward curves.

5 Turn the stitched fabric right side out, position and attach any ears with slipstitches and fill with fibrefill, as shown in figure 3.

6 Sew up the opening with slipstitches, tucking the seam allowances neatly inside.

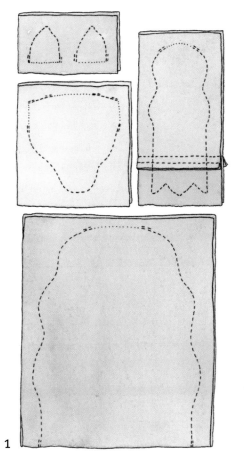

1

2

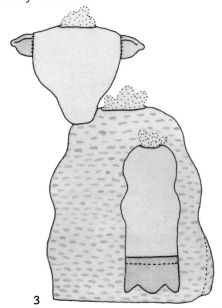

3

Folded strap

1 Cut a strip of fabric to the measurements given in the pattern instructions.
2 Fold and press the strip as shown in figure 1a.
3 Topstitch just 2mm (1/16in) from the edge as shown in figure 1b.

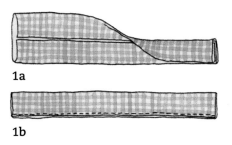

1a

1b

Attaching a zip

The zip should have a length at least equal to that of the piece or pieces of fabric on to which it will be sewn. It is fine if it is longer – the section that is too long can be cut off when the zip has been joined to the fabric(s).

1 Place the closed zip to the fabric edge with right sides facing and sew, taking a presser foot's seam allowance (see figure 1).
2 Turn the zip right side up and topstitch the seam 3–4mm (1/8in) from the zip (see figure 2).
3 Place the zip right sides together with the second piece of fabric as shown in figure 3 and sew, taking a presser foot's seam allowance.
4 Topstitch the seam allowance as shown in figure 4.

Cushion pad

If it is not possible to buy a cushion pad of the required size, you can easily make one as described here:

1 Cut the fabric to the measurements given in the pattern, or calculate what size the finished cushion should be: twice the height plus 1.5cm (5/8in) by the width plus 1.5cm (5/8in).
2 Fold the fabric in half with right sides together and sew, taking a presser foot's seam allowance and leaving an opening of about 12cm (4¾in) as shown in figure 5.
3 Turn out the fabric through the opening, stuff the cushion with fibrefill and sew up the opening with slipstitches.

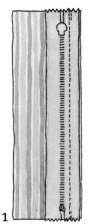

1

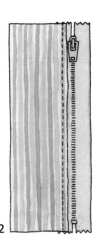

2

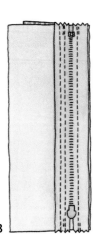

3

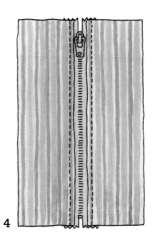

4

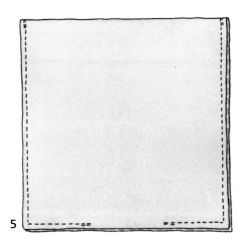

5

Slipstitch

Slipstitches are used for sewing up openings, for example. They are worked by hand and sewn from right to left (see figure 1).

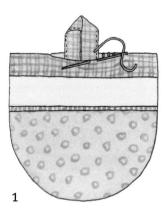

1

Blind-hemming stitch

Blind-hemming stitches are similar to slipstitches, but you should try to get the stitch underneath the part to be appliquéd, making the stitch invisible (see figure 2).

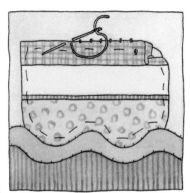

2

Overcast stitch

These stitches are used when two raw edges need to be joined (see figure 3).

3

Running stitch and quilting stitch

Running stitch and quilting stitch are both sewn from right to left. Running stitches can be used for facial expressions and are sewn on to a single layer of fabric.

Quilting stitches are sewn as regular stitches through the front side, the interlining and the back of the quilt layers. Alternate stitches are visible on the front and back (see figure 4).

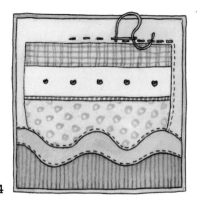

4

French knots

Many of the animals in this book have eyes that are sewn with French knots. The size of the knot depends on how many times the thread is circled around the needle. The needle is inserted back down close to where it emerged. It is important to tighten the thread before inserting the needle through the fabric (see figure 5).

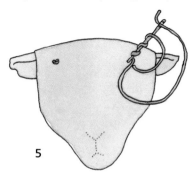

5

Backstitch

Backstitches are used in this book to sew facial expressions. The needle is inserted behind the point where it emerged, as shown in figure 6.

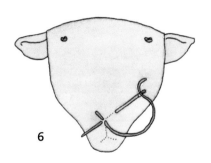

6

Noah and his Wife

These cloth dolls are 90cm (35½in) tall and stuffed with fibrefill but with a small bag inside each one filled with pellets to help them sit up properly. They are made from the same set of patterns, but they are otherwise quite different. Noah is explained first; he is in work clothes and has a small model of the Ark under his arm. The instructions for making Noah's wife begin on page 19.

The patterns are provided on pages 23–27 and should be extended where indicated.

Noah

For the pattern, see page 23.

Materials:
Skin-coloured fabric for the body and arms: 35 x 45cm (13¾ x 17¾in)
Fabric for the long underwear: 45 x 60cm (17¾ x 23½in)
Fabric for the boots: 10.5 x 45cm (4 x 17¾in)
Fabric for the pellet bag: 12 x 20cm (4¾ x 8in)
Fibrefill
Pellets

1 Draw the pattern pieces full size.
2 Cut a piece of skin-coloured fabric 23 x 30cm (9 x 12in) and a piece of underwear fabric 20 x 23cm (8 x 9in).
3 Sew them together with right sides facing along the edge measuring 23cm (9in).

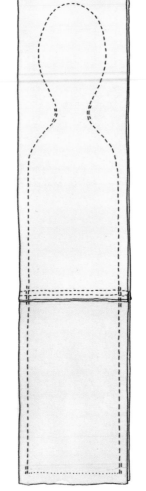
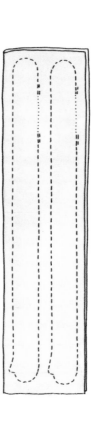
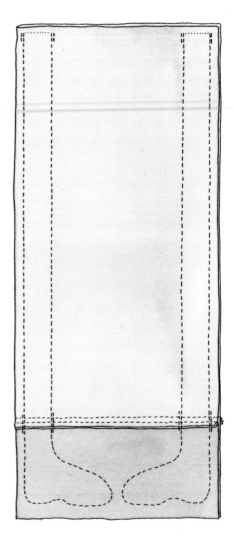

1

4 Fold the seam allowances down against the underwear fabric and topstitch it in place.
5 Fold the joined piece right sides together, draw the body on top and sew along the drawn line, leaving an opening at the bottom of the body (see figure 1).

6 Cut out the body, adding a 3mm (⅛in) seam allowance all round. Trim off the seam allowance at the bottom, straight edge. Turn right side out.
7 Fold the remaining skin-coloured fabric right sides together, so the short side is halved.

8 Draw two arms on top and sew along the line, leaving an opening on each one as marked on the pattern (see figure 1 on page 12).

9 Cut out the arms, adding a 3mm (⅛in) seam allowance all round except at the openings where it should be 5mm (¼in). Turn right side out.

10 Sew the boot fabric right sides together with the remaining underwear fabric. Press the seam allowances towards the boot fabric and topstitch it in place.

11 Fold the joined piece right sides together, draw two legs on top as shown in figure 1 on page 12 and sew along the line, leaving an opening at the top of the leg.

12 Cut out the legs, adding a 3mm (⅛in) seam allowance all round except at the opening where you should cut along the line. Turn right side out.

13 Stuff the arms and legs firmly with fibrefill up to 12cm (4¾in) and 17cm (6¾in) respectively and thereafter stuff loosely.

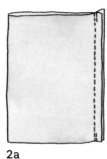

2a

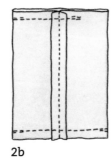

2b

14 Sew up the opening of the arms with slipstitches and quilt the fingers as marked on the pattern (see page 11).

15 Sew the pellet bag with an opening as shown in figures 2a and 2b, turn the bag right side out, fill it with pellets and sew up the opening with slipstitches.

16 Position the legs right sides together with the front of the body and sew them in place, taking a presser foot's seam allowance all around the bottom of the body – this provides a marker along which the seam allowance can be folded.

17 Now stuff the head and body very firmly – be especially thorough at the neck. Leave room in the body for the pellet bag.

18 Tuck in the seam allowance on the body and sew up the opening with slipstitches.

Trousers

For the pattern, see page 24.

Materials:
Fabric: 60 x 60cm (23½ x 23½in)

1 Draw the pattern pieces full size.

2 Cut two trouser legs on the fold as marked on the pattern.

3 Put the legs right sides together, sew the centre-front (CF) seam, cut notches in the curve and zigzag the raw edges together (see figure 1).

1

4 Zigzag the trouser waist and leg ends separately (see figure 1).

5 Cut a 17 x 25cm (6¾ x 10in) piece of trouser fabric for the pockets and fold it as shown in figure 2a.

6 Draw two back pockets and two front pockets and stitch as shown.

7 Cut out the pockets, adding a 3mm (⅛in) seam allowance all round. Turn right side out and stitch as shown in figure 2b.

8 Cut a piece of fabric 3 x 7cm (1¼ x 2¾in) for a strap. Fold and sew the strap as explained on page 10.

9 Position the front pockets 5cm (2in) from the top edge of the trousers and 7.5mm (a generous ¼in) from the centre front.

10 Position the back pockets 5cm (2in) from the top edge of the trousers and 1cm (⅜in) from the front pockets.

11 Position the strap between one front and one back pocket (see figure 3).

12 Topstitch the pockets in place, 1–2mm (¹⁄₁₆in) from the edge.

13 Press 2cm (¾in) over towards the wrong side along the top and bottom edges and then open back out.

14 With right sides facing, stitch the centre-back (CB) edge as explained in step 3.

15 Refold and stitch the waistband and leg hems with two rows of topstitches, as shown in figure 4.

16 Match the centre-front and centre-back seams, right sides together and sew the inside-leg seam from hem to hem. Cut notches in the curve and zigzag the raw edges together. Turn the trousers right side out.

17 Put the trousers on the body, make a couple of small pleats at the trouser waist to fit and attach the trousers to the body at the waist with slipstitches.

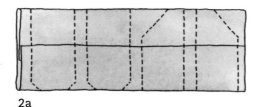

2a

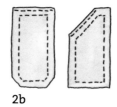

2b

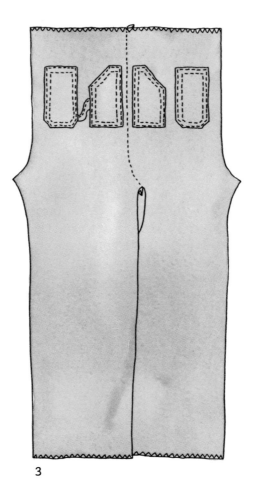

3

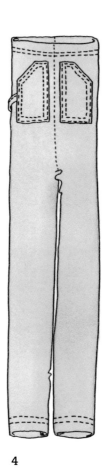

4

Shirt

For the pattern, see pages 24–25.

Materials:

Fabric: 28 x 90cm (11 x 35½in)
Five or six small buttons for the front
Two buttons for the arms

1 Draw the pattern pieces full size.
2 Cut two front pieces on the fold and one back piece on the fold.
3 Fold the remaining fabric right sides together and draw two sleeves.
4 Sew the bottom edges and necklines of the front pieces (see figure 1a).
5 Trim the seam allowance back to 3mm (⅛in), turn right side out and topstitch the front pieces 5–7.5mm (¼in) from the edge (see figure 1b).
6 Zigzag the lower edge of the back piece, fold 7.5mm (¼in) towards the wrong side and topstitch it in place.

7 Mark a hem allowance of 7.5mm (a generous ¼in) along the neckline and cut 7–8 small notches in as far as the marked line.
8 Press the hem towards the wrong side and topstitch it in place (see figure 2).
9 Place the front pieces right sides together with the back piece and sew the side seams. Trim the seam allowance back to 4mm (⅛in).
10 Zigzag the raw edges together, as shown in figure 3.
11 Mark the position of five or six buttons on the centre-front (CF) line, put the shirt on Noah and sew the buttons in place through both front pieces.
12 Sew the sleeves along the drawn line then cut out, adding 4mm (⅛in) seam allowances all round. Zigzag the edges together, if desired.

13 Using a marking needle, mark a fold line 4.5cm (1¾in) from the lower edge of the sleeve, as shown in figure 4.
14 Turn the sleeves right side out and fold under 4.5cm (1¾in) on each sleeve.
15 Roll up the sleeves and secure the roll-up with slipstitches.
16 Pull the sleeves on the arms and sew them in place on the body with buttons, which are sewn through the body from arm to arm (see figure 5).

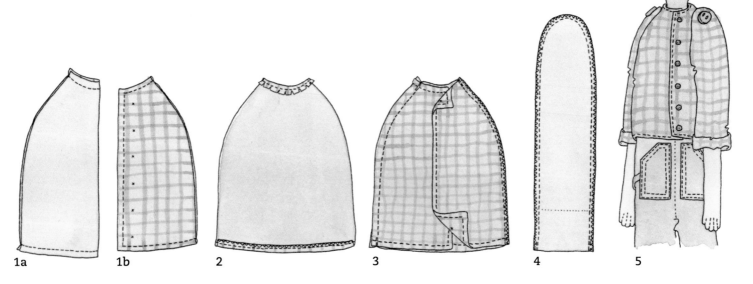

1a   1b   2   3   4   5

Waistcoat

For the pattern, see page 25.

Materials:
Fabric: 20 x 75cm (8 x 29½in)
Two buttons

1 Cut two back pieces on the fold as marked on the pattern and four front pieces.
2 Put two of the front pieces right sides together with each back piece. Sew the side seams and press the seam allowances open.
3 Place the two waistcoats right sides together and sew as shown in figure 1.
4 Trim the seam allowances back to 3mm (⅛in) and cut small notches into the seam allowances at the neck, armholes and centre-back vent.
5 Turn the waistcoat right side out, put the right sides of the shoulders together, fold down the lining of the front pieces and sew, taking a presser foot's seam allowance through the other three layers as shown in figure 2 (left-hand side).
6 Stuff the three seam allowances into the waistcoat.
7 Fold the seam allowance on the lining towards the wrong side, so the stitching is just covered, and sew the shoulders with slipstitches as shown in figure 2 (right-hand side).
8 Turn the waistcoat right side out and topstitch the edge (see figure 3).
9 Sew two buttons on one front piece as marked on the pattern and stitch buttonholes to correspond on the other front piece.

Beret

For the pattern, see page 25.

Materials:
Felt: 8.5 x 17cm (3½ x 6¾in)

1 Fold the felt right sides together and draw the large and small circles centrally on top.
2 Cut out the small circle in the upper layer of felt only and sew through both layers around the large circle (see figure 1).
3 Cut outside the large circle, adding a 3mm (⅛in) seam allowance, then turn right side out.
4 Roll a small 'stalk' from a short strip of felt and sew it in place in the middle of the beret.
5 Position the beret on Noah's head, put a little tousled thread under the edge of the beret for hair and sew the beret in place with slipstitches.
6 Clip the hair to length.
7 Sew the eyes with French knots and the mouth with running stitches or backstitches.

2

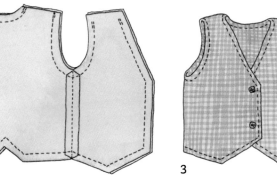

1

3

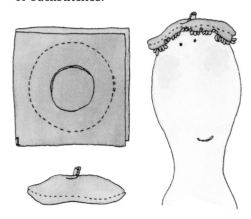

1

The Ark

The Ark, which Noah holds, is approximately 12 x 14cm (4¾ x 5½in), and it can be filled about halfway up with pellets, so it can stand without support and be used, for example, as a pincushion.
For the pattern, see page 26.

Materials:
Fabric for the roof: 6.5 x 16cm (2½ x 6¼in)
Fabric for the house: two pieces 4.5 x 16cm (1¾ x 6¼in)
Fabric for the boat: two pieces 10 x 16cm (4 x 6¼in)
Fusible wadding: 16 x 30cm (6¼ x 12in)
Fabric for the gunwale: 2 x 31cm (¾ x 12¼in)
Five buttons for the portholes
Fibrefill
Some pellets, if desired, about 150ml (10 tablespoons)

1 Sew the fabric strips for the house right sides together with the roof as shown in figure 1. Using an iron, press the seam allowance towards the roof.
2 Sew the fabric strips for the boat right sides together with the house, leaving an opening in one seam as shown in figure 2.
3 Press the seam allowances open.
4 Cut the fusible wadding into two pieces, 9.5 x 16cm (3¾ x 6¼in) and 20.5 x 16cm (8¼ x 6¼in). Iron the pieces on to the wrong side of the fabrics, as shown in figure 3.
5 Topstitch the roof's seam allowances in place.
6 Fold the piece right sides together, transfer the pattern and sew along the drawn pattern line as shown in figure 4.

7 Cut out the Ark, adding a 3mm (⅛in) seam allowance all round. Turn right side out.
8 Stuff the Ark firmly with fibrefill and, if the Ark is to stand by itself, fill the bottom with pellets.
9 Sew up the opening with slipstitches.
10 Fold the gunwale as shown in figure 5 and position it over the join between house and boat.
11 Appliqué the gunwale in place.
12 Lastly, sew on the buttons as portholes.

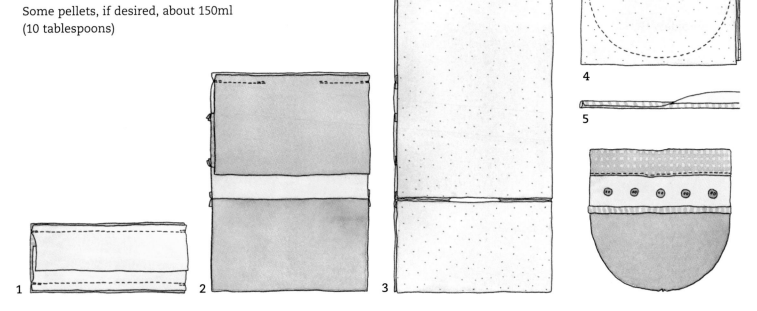

1

2

3

4

5

Noah's wife

Noah's wife, who is in her Sunday best, is sewn basically in the same way as Noah. However, she is wearing pantalettes so there are differences in how the fabrics are cut and sewn together.

For the pattern, see page 23.

Materials:

Skin-coloured fabric for the body, arms
   and legs: 45 x 75cm (17½ x 29½in)
Fabric for the shirt: 23 x 65cm
   (9 x 25½in)
Fabric for the pantalettes: 20 x 35cm
   (8 x 13¾in)
Fabric for the shoes: 7.5 x 45cm
   (3 x 17¾in)
Fabric for the pellet bag: 12 x 20cm
   (4¾ x 8in)
Fibrefill
Pellets
DMC embroidery thread for hair

1 Draw the pattern full size.
2 Cut a piece of skin-coloured fabric 23 x 30cm (9 x 12in) and a piece of pantalette fabric 20 x 23cm (8 x 9in).
3 Sew the fabrics together with right sides facing along the sides that measure 23cm (9in).
4 Fold the seam allowance towards the pantalette fabric and topstitch in place.
5 Fold the piece right sides together and draw the body pattern on top.
6 Sew along the drawn line, leaving an opening at the bottom (see figure 1, page 12).

7 Cut out the body, adding a 3mm (⅛in) seam allowance all round. Trim off the seam allowance at the bottom, straight edge. Turn right side out.
8 Cut a piece of skin-coloured fabric 10 x 20cm (4 x 8in) and a piece of shirt fabric 20 x 26cm (8 x 10¼in) and sew them right sides together along the sides that measure 20cm (8in). The remaining shirt fabric will be used for a shirt/jacket combination (see page 21).
9 Press the seam allowance on to the shirt-fabric side and topstitch it in place.
10 Fold the piece right sides together, draw two arms on top and sew along the drawn line, leaving an opening on each arm as marked on the pattern (see figure 1).
11 Cut out the arms, adding a 3mm (⅛in) seam allowance all round except at the opening, where you should add 5mm (¼in). Turn right side out.
12 Cut a piece of skin-coloured fabric 43 x 45cm (17 x 17¾in) and sew it right sides together with the shoe fabric along the sides that measure 45cm (17¾in).
13 Press the seam allowances towards the shoe fabric and topstitch in place.
14 Fold the piece right sides together, draw two legs and sew along the drawn line, leaving an opening at the top of the legs (see figure 1, page 12).
15 Cut out, adding a 3mm (⅛in) seam allowance all round. Trim off the seam allowance at the opening.

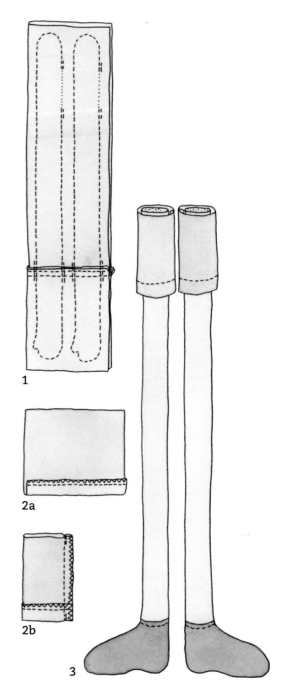

1

2a

2b

3

16 Cut two pantalette legs, each 10 x 10.5cm (4 x 4⅛in).

17 Zigzag along one long side as shown in figure 2a. Fold 1.5cm (⅝in) over towards the wrong side and sew the fold in place.

18 Fold the piece right sides together as shown in figure 2b.

19 Sew together, taking a presser foot's seam allowance, as shown, and zigzag the raw edges together. Turn right side out.

20 Sew the other pantalette leg in the same way.

21 Put the pantalette legs on the model's legs (see figure 3).

22 Sew a pellet bag as shown in figure 2a and 2b on page 14.

23 Stuff the arms and legs firmly with fibrefill, up to 12cm (4¾in) and 17cm (6¾in) respectively, and thereafter stuff loosely.

24 Sew up the openings on the arms with slipstitches and quilt the fingers as marked on the pattern (see page 11).

25 Position the legs right sides together with the front body piece and sew the legs in place, taking a presser foot's seam allowance around the bottom of the body – this provides a marker along which the seam allowance can be folded.

26 Now stuff the head and body very firmly – be especially thorough at the neck. Leave room in the body for the pellet bag.

27 Tuck the seam allowance on the body towards the wrong side and sew up the opening with slipstitches.

28 Sew the eyes with French knots and the mouth with running stitches or backstitches.

29 Cut 20–25 threads of DMC embroidery thread each 35cm (13¾in) long and sew them along the crown as shown in figure 4. 'Lock' each thread by putting both ends through the loop.

30 Comb the hair back smoothly and then sew a row of backstitches (see figure 5). The hair can now be plaited and twisted into a bun, or just twisted into a bun.

31 Sew the bun in place using thread to match the hair.

Skirt

Materials:
Fabric: 52 x 55cm (20½ x 21¾in)
1cm (⅜in) wide elastic to fit the waist

1 Zigzag the edges of the fabric and press a 3cm (1¼in) hem towards the wrong side at the top and a 2cm (¾in) hem towards the wrong side at the bottom. The piece should now measure 47 x 55cm (18½ x 21¾in).

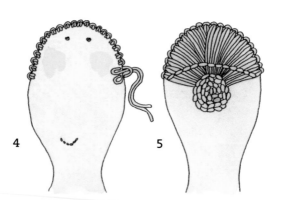

4   5

2 Open the hems, fold the piece right sides together and sew the centre-back (CB) seam. Press the seam allowances open.

3 Fold the top hem and sew two rows of stitches, 1.5cm (⅝in) apart, for a drawstring channel. Leave a small opening in the lowest row of stitching, so you can thread the elastic through the channel (see the illustration, below).

4 Fold the bottom hem and sew in place.

5 Thread the elastic through the drawstring hem and join the ends.

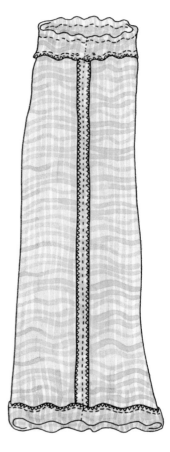

Shirt and jacket combination

The shirt and jacket are sewn together into a so-called 'cheat shirt' – the shirt has two fronts but shares the same back piece as the jacket.

For the pattern, see pages 24–25.

Materials:

Fabric for the jacket: 50 x 55cm (19¾ x 21¾in)

Leftover fabric from the body for the shirt

Four or five small buttons for the front

Two buttons for the arms

1 Draw the pattern full size.

2 Fold the shirt fabric (which was left over when the body was sewn) right sides together and cut two front pieces on the fold as marked on the pattern.

3 Sew along the neck and bottom edges, taking a presser foot's seam allowance (see figure 1a on page 16). Trim the seam allowance back to 3mm (⅛in).

4 Turn right side out and topstitch the edges, if desired.

5 Mark the position of 4 or 5 buttons on the centre-front line (see figure 1b on page 16).

6 Cut and sew two front pieces in the jacket fabric as just explained, without marking for buttons.

7 Cut a back piece on the fold in the jacket fabric. Zigzag the bottom edge, fold 7.5mm (a generous ¼in) to the wrong side and sew the hem.

8 Mark a seam allowance along the neckline and cut 5 or 6 notches in the seam allowance.

9 Fold and press the seam allowances towards the wrong side and topstitch the hem in place (see figure 2 on page 16).

10 Put the front pieces of the jacket right sides together with the back and add the front pieces of the shirt, right sides facing the wrong side of the jacket piece.

11 Sew the side seams, trim the seam allowance back to 4mm (a generous ⅛in) and zigzag the raw edges together (see figure 1).

12 Turn the jacket/shirt right side out, put it on Noah's wife and sew the buttons in place through both front pieces of the shirt.

13 Cut a piece of jacket fabric 23 x 30cm (9 x 12in) for the sleeves and zigzag along one long edge (the hem edge).

14 Fold 1.5cm (⅝in) towards the wrong side and sew the hem in place.

15 Fold the fabric right sides together and draw two sleeves as shown in figure 2. Stitch along the drawn lines.

16 Cut out the sleeves, adding a 3mm (⅛in) seam allowance and turn right side out.

17 Put the sleeves on the arms and sew them in place on the body with buttons, which are sewn through the body from arm to arm (see the illustration below).

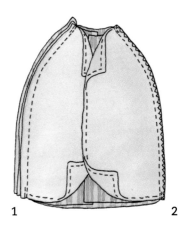

1

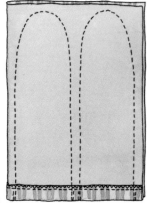

2

The dove

Despite its size, the dove has a significant role in the story of Noah's Ark. It is roughly 7 x 12cm (2¾ x 4¾in). For the pattern, see page 26.

Materials:
Fabric for the body: 13 x 19cm (5 x 7½in)
Fabric for the wing: 10 x 14cm (4 x 5½in)
Fabric for the tail: 7 x 9cm (2¾ x 3½in)
Fabric for the beak: 5 x 5cm (2 x 2in)
Soft fusible interfacing (optional)
Fibrefill
Two small beads for the eyes (optional)

1 Iron soft interfacing on to the wrong side of the fabrics, if necessary.
2 Fold the pieces of fabric for the body, wing and tail right sides together and draw the appropriate pattern on each one.
3 Cut out the body, adding a 1cm (⅜in) seam allowance (see figure 1).
4 Fold 7.5mm (a generous ¼in) towards the wrong side all round the beak fabric and tack in place.
5 Fold the beak fabric in half diagonally (only one triangle will be used).
6 Position the triangular beak piece on the body as shown in figure 2 and appliqué it in place.
7 Sew the wing and tail pieces together in pairs with right sides facing, leaving openings as marked (see page 9).

8 Turn the parts right side out and sew up the opening on the wing with slipstitches.
9 Quilt stitch 2mm (1/16in) in on both the wing and the tail and stuff a little fibrefill into the tail.
10 Position the wing as shown in figure 2 and sew it in place.
11 Fold the body fabric right sides together and sew along the drawn line along the dove's belly, leaving an opening as shown in figure 3.
12 Trim the seam allowance back to 3mm (⅛in) along the belly but leave 5mm (¼in) at the opening.

13 Arrange the dove's rear (open) end so the seam allowance for the belly lies over the fold on the back (see figure 4).
14 Position the tail in the opening and sew it in place, taking a presser foot's seam allowance.
15 Trim the seam allowance back to 3mm (¼in).
16 Turn the dove right side out, stuff it firmly with fibrefill and sew up the opening with slipstitches.
17 Sew the eyes with French knots or, better still, with small beads.

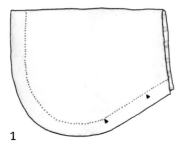

1

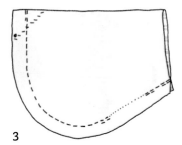

2

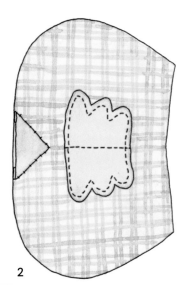

3

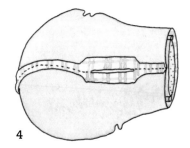

4

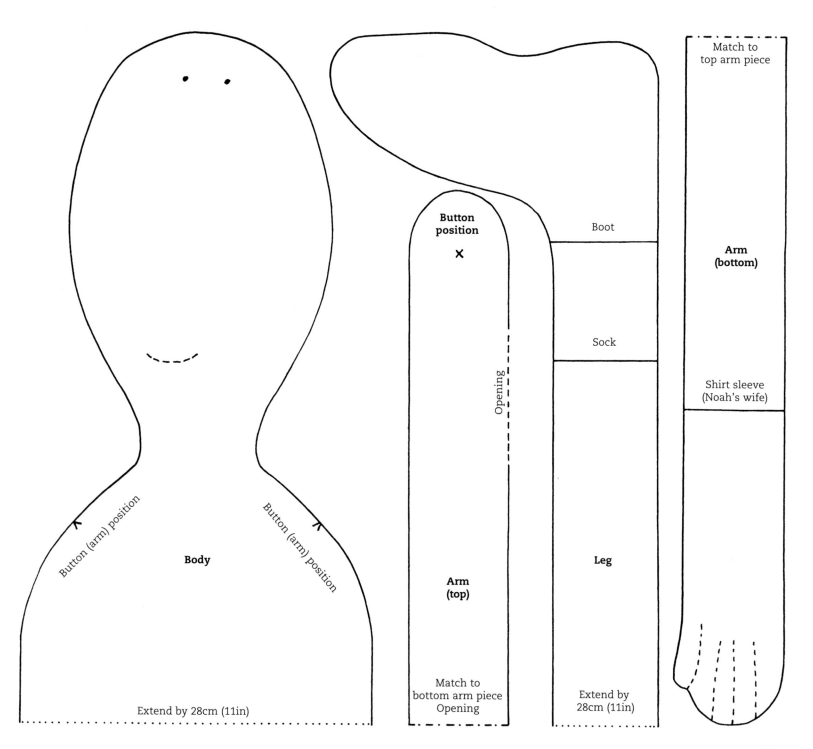

Body

Button (arm) position

Button (arm) position

Extend by 28cm (11in)

Button
position

✗

Opening

Arm
(top)

Match to
bottom arm piece
Opening

Boot

Sock

Leg

Extend by
28cm (11in)

Match to
top arm piece

Arm
(bottom)

Shirt sleeve
(Noah's wife)

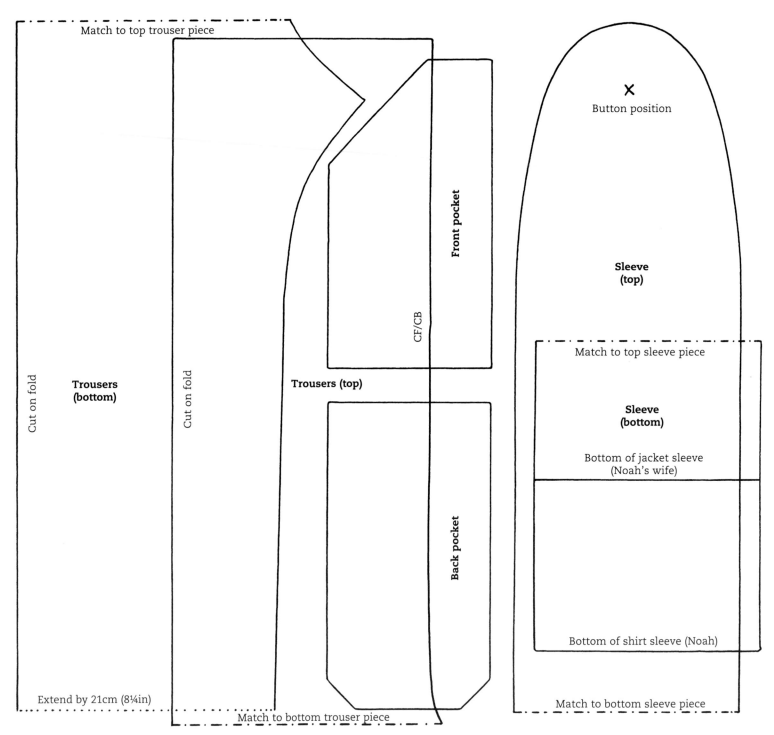

Match to top trouser piece

**Trousers
(bottom)**

Cut on fold

Cut on fold

Trousers (top)

Front pocket

CF/CB

Back pocket

Extend by 21cm (8¼in)

Match to bottom trouser piece

✗

Button position

**Sleeve
(top)**

Match to top sleeve piece

**Sleeve
(bottom)**

Bottom of jacket sleeve
(Noah's wife)

Bottom of shirt sleeve (Noah)

Match to bottom sleeve piece

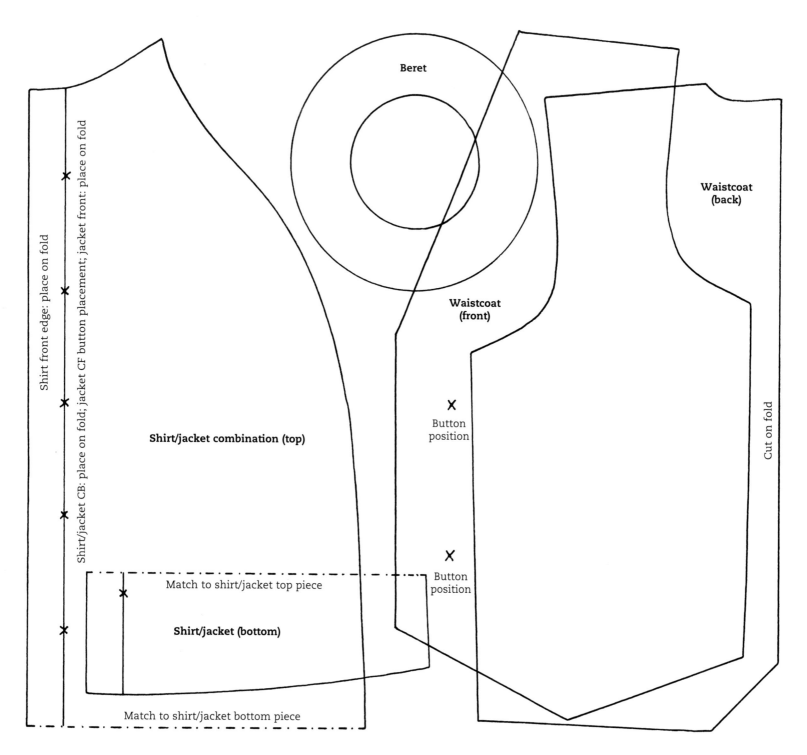

Shirt front edge: place on fold

Shirt/jacket CB: place on fold; jacket CF button placement; jacket front: place on fold

Beret

Waistcoat (back)

Waistcoat (front)

Shirt/jacket combination (top)

Cut on fold

✗ Button position

✗ Button position

Match to shirt/jacket top piece

✗

Shirt/jacket (bottom)

Match to shirt/jacket bottom piece

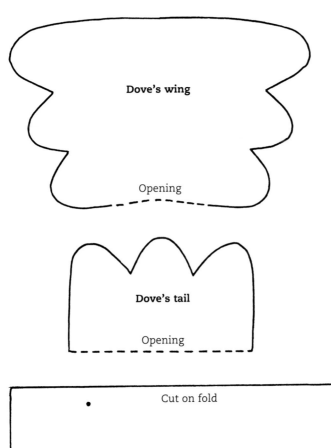

Dove's wing

Opening

Dove's tail

Opening

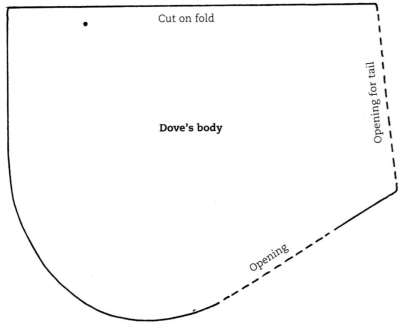

Cut on fold

Dove's body

Opening for tail

Opening

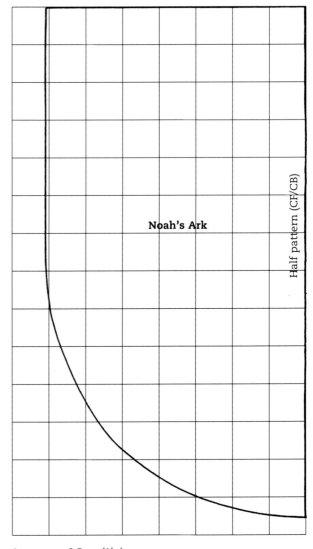

Noah's Ark

Half pattern (CF/CB)

1 square = 2.5cm (1in)

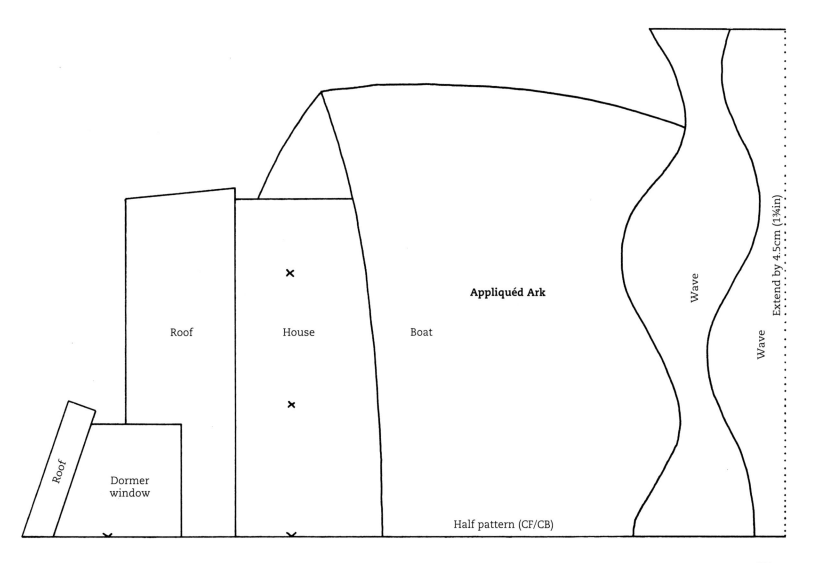

Roof

House

Boot

Appliquéd Ark

Wave

Wave

Extend by 4.5cm (1¾in)

Roof

Dormer
window

Half pattern (CF/CB)

27

Appliquéd Ark

This small quilt hanging is 33 x 33cm (13 x 13in). For the pattern, see page 27.

Materials:
Assorted fabric remnants for the appliqué
Fabric for the gunwale: 1.5 x 40cm (⅝ x 16in)
Fabric for the front panel (sky): 30 x 30cm (12 x 12in)
Fabric for the back: 35 x 35cm (13¾ x 13¾in)
Fabric for the frame: 6 x 125cm (2⅜ x 49¼in)
Fabric for the hanging sleeve: 9.5 x 35cm (3¾ x 13¾in)
Fabric for binding: 6.25 x 140cm (2½ x 55in)
Wadding: 35 x 35cm (13¾ x 13¾in)
Six buttons for portholes

1 Draw the picture full size and cut it apart along the drawn lines.
2 Draw all the parts of the Ark on the wrong side of the appropriate fabrics, adding 5–7.5mm (¼in) seam allowances all around.
3 Cut out the pieces.
4 Fold the seam allowances towards the wrong side and tack in place – if part of a pattern piece is going to lie under another piece, you do not have to fold the seam allowance under at that edge.
5 Fold the gunwale fabric, as shown in figure 5 on page 18.

6 Cut off two short pieces of gunwale, each 4.5cm (1¾in) long, and position them with one end under the house.
7 Position and tack each part of the front fabric.
8 Appliqué the Ark on to the front. Appliqué the long gunwale section on so that it covers the transition between the house and boat, folding the ends under.
9 Trim the front panel so that it measures approximately 27 x 27cm (10½ x 10½in).
10 Sew 6cm (2⅜in) framing strips around the picture as shown in the final illustration on page 30. The strips can be placed so the waves reach all the way out to the edge.
11 Place the front and back pieces wrong sides together with the wadding in between, tack the layers together and trim the edges so the piece measures approximately 33 x 33cm (13 x 13in).
12 Quilt as shown in the final illustration on page 30.
13 Fold the short ends of the fabric for the hanging sleeve 3.5cm (1⅜in) towards the wrong side and sew as shown in figure 1.
14 Press a sharp fold 4cm (1½in) down from one long edge as shown.
15 Position the sleeve on the back of the picture, so the raw edges are flush with the upper edge of the picture and there is equal distance at the sides. Tack, if desired (see figure 2).

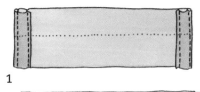

1

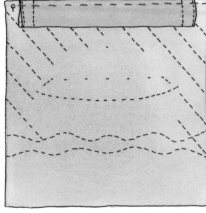

2

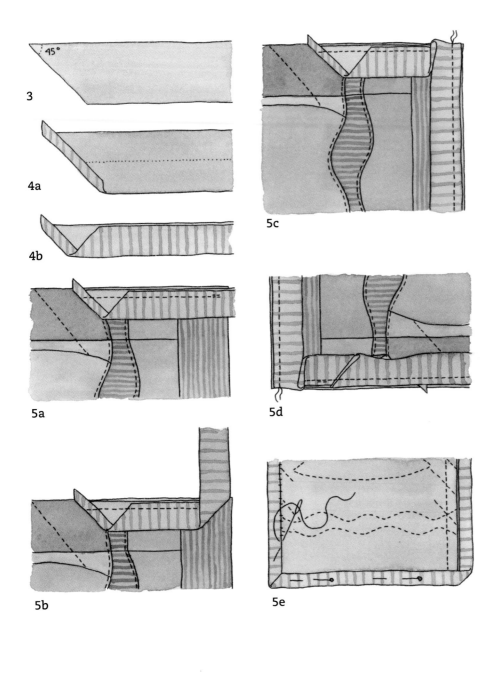

3

4a

4b

5a

5b

5c

5d

5e

16 Cut off the ends of the binding fabric obliquely as shown in figure 3.
17 Fold a seam allowance along the slanted edge then fold the strip wrong sides together and press (see figures 4a and 4b).
18 Sew the binding to the front of the appliqué with right sides together, as shown in figures 5a–5c. When the starting point is reached, cut the strip off obliquely, so it overlaps by 1.5cm (⅝in), then sew it in place (see figure 5d).
19 Fold the edge of the binding over to the back of the piece and sew it in place with slipstitches (see figure 5e). Be careful not to stitch through to the front.

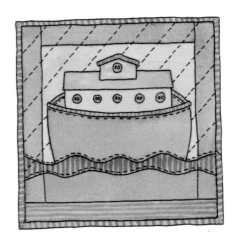

Small Animals

These charming little animals go well with the appliquéd Ark (page 28) and the Ark cushion (page 38). To make the animals stand properly, some pellets are added to the body before it is stuffed with fibrefill.

The models can also be sewn as flat animals. To do this, simply draw the models 1.25cm (½in) shorter.

For the patterns, see pages 36–37.

Materials:
Fabric
Pellets
Fibrefill
A button for each rabbit

Body

1 Draw the chosen half-body pattern full size.
2 Fold the fabric right sides together and draw the body pattern on top. Sew all round, leaving an opening as indicated on the pattern. Do not turn the body right side out yet.

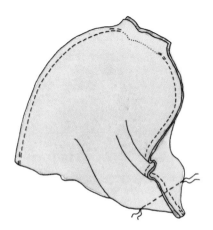

3 Lay one side seam over the bottom fold of the body and sew across the corner as shown in the illustration below. The seam should be 2.5–3cm (1–1¼in) long.
4 Sew the other bottom corner in the same way.
5 Turn the body right side out. Put approximately three tablespoons of pellets inside and then stuff firmly with fibrefill. Slipstitch the opening closed.

Cats

For the pattern, see page 36.

1 Make the body as just explained.
2 Sew the head, ears, legs and tail pieces together in pairs with right sides facing; turn out and stuff (see page 9). Position the ears on the head and sew them in place.
3 Close up the openings on the legs and tail, tucking the seam allowances inside, then quilt the legs as illustrated.

4 Sew the eyes with French knots and the facial features with long backstitches.
5 Position the head, legs and tail and appliqué the parts in place.

Rabbits

For the pattern, see page 36.

1 Make the body as just explained.
2 Sew the head, ears and legs together in pairs with right sides facing; turn out and stuff (see page 9). Position the ears on the head and sew them in place.
3 Close up the openings on the legs, tucking the seam allowances inside, then quilt the front legs as illustrated.
4 Sew the eyes with French knots and the facial features with backstitches.
5 Position the head and front legs and appliqué the parts in place. Attach the hind leg with a button.

Hens

For the pattern, see page 36.

1 Make the body as explained on page 31 but do not close up the body opening.

2 Sew the tail-feather piece as explained on page 9. Turn it out and stuff it then position it in the body opening and sew it up with slipstitches.

3 Sew the head, comb and wattle (for the cockerel) pieces as explained on page 9, turn them out and stuff them. Position the comb in the head opening and sew it up with slipstitches.

4 Cut a piece of fabric 3 x 3cm (1¼ x 1¼in) for the beak, fold it diagonally and sew, taking a 5mm (¼in) seam allowance along two sides as shown in figure 1a.

5 Cut a slit to turn through in the back then turn out and fill the beak lightly. Oversew the slit edges (see figure 1b).

6 Position the beak and sew it in place with slipstitches. Attach the head to the body. The lightly stuffed wattle on the cockerel should be sewn in place under the beak with overcast stitches.

Geese

For the pattern, see page 36.

1 Make the body as explained on page 31.

2 Sew the head, beak and feet with right sides facing as explained on page 9. Turn out and stuff the pieces. Figures 2a and 2b show how the beak is stitched, turned through a slit cut on the back, lightly stuffed and then the slit is oversewn.

3 Attach the head to the body.

4 Sew nasal openings and a small smile on the goose's beak before positioning it and appliquéing it in place.

5 Fold the feet as shown in figure 3 and sew them in place under the body with slipstitches.

6 Sew the eyes with French knots.

1a

1b

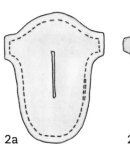

2a

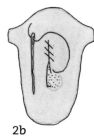

2b

3

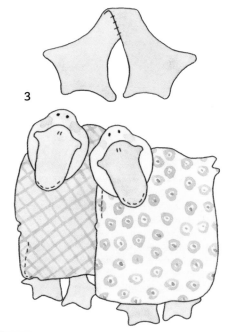

Sitting sheep

For the pattern, see page 37.

1 Make the body as explained on page 31.
2 Sew the head and ear pieces together in pairs (see page 9). Turn out and stuff them. Attach the ears to the head.
3 Sew the eyes with French knots and the nose/mouth with backstitches.
4 Cut fabric rectangles 8 x 10cm (3¼ x 4in) for the legs and 3.5 x 10cm (1½ x 4in) for the hooves.
5 Stitch the pieces right sides together along one 10cm (4in) edge.
6 Press the seam allowances towards the hoof fabric and topstitch in place.
7 Fold the piece right sides together, draw the legs on top, sew, turn out and stuff. Tuck the seam allowances inside at the opening and slipstitch closed.
8 Quilt the line between the legs as illustrated.
9 Position the head and legs and appliqué them on to the body.

Standing sheep

For the pattern, see page 37.

1 Sew the body, head, ears and the two oblong leg pieces together as described on page 9. The leg pieces should be loosely stuffed near the openings. Position the ears and sew them in place.
2 Fold the leg pieces in the middle, so there are two sets of two legs.
3 Position the legs in the body openings and sew them in place with slipstitches.
4 Sew the eyes with French knots and the nose/mouth with backstitches. Appliqué the head in place.

Pigs

For the pattern, see page 37.

1 Make the body as explained on page 31.
2 Sew the head, snout and ears together in pairs; turn out and stuff (see page 9). Position the ears and sew them in place. The snout is turned through a small slit cut on the back, just like the goose's beak (see page 32).
3 Quilt the snout 2mm (¹⁄₁₆in) from the edge and sew the nostrils with French knots.
4 Appliqué the snout to the head and sew the eyes with French knots.
5 Cut fabric rectangles 8 x 10cm (3¼ x 4in) for the legs and 3.5 x 10cm (1½ x 4in) for the trotters.
6 Sew the pieces together with right sides facing along one 10cm (4in) edge.

7 Press the seam allowances towards the trotter fabric and topstitch in place.

8 Fold the piece right sides together, draw the legs on top, stitch, turn out and stuff. Tuck in the seam allowances at the opening and slipstitch closed.

9 Quilt the line between the legs as illustrated.

10 Position the head and legs and appliqué them on to the body.

11 Cut a strip 1 x 9cm (⅜ x 3½in) for the tail.

12 Fold and press the tail strip as shown in figure 1.

13 Open the fold, fray 1cm (⅜in) of fabric at one end and fold the seam allowance to the wrong side at the other end.

14 Refold the tail and sew it together with slipstitches or running stitches.

15 Sew the tail to the body and curl it into shape.

1

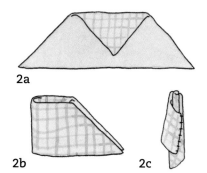

2a

2b   2c

Cows

For the pattern, see page 37.

1 Make the body as explained on page 31.

2 Sew the head, muzzle and ears together in pairs with right sides facing; turn out and stuff. Position the ears and sew them in place. The muzzle should be turned through a small slit cut on the back, just like the goose's beak (see page 32).

3 Cut a piece of fabric 4 x 4cm (1½ x 1½in) for the bull's horns, cut it diagonally and fold and roll the horns as shown in figures 2a–2c.

4 Secure the rolls with slipstitches.

5 Position the horns between the sides of the top head opening and sew them in place at the same time as sewing up the opening.

6 Sew nostrils on the muzzle as marked on the pattern.

7 Appliqué the muzzle on to the head and sew the eyes with French knots. You could add backstitches around the eyes to make them bigger.

8 Cut fabric pieces 10 x 10cm (4 x 4in) for the legs and 3.5 x 10cm (1½ x 4in) for the hooves and sew them as explained for the pig.

9 Quilt the legs as illustrated.

10 Position the head and legs and appliqué them on to the body.

11 Cut a 1.5 x 10cm (⅝ x 4in) strip for the tail and sew it as explained for the pig.

12 Position the tail on the body and sew it in place.

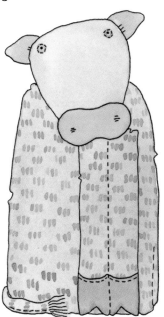

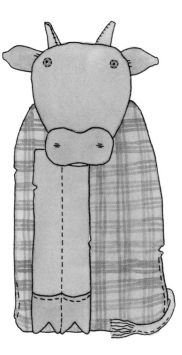

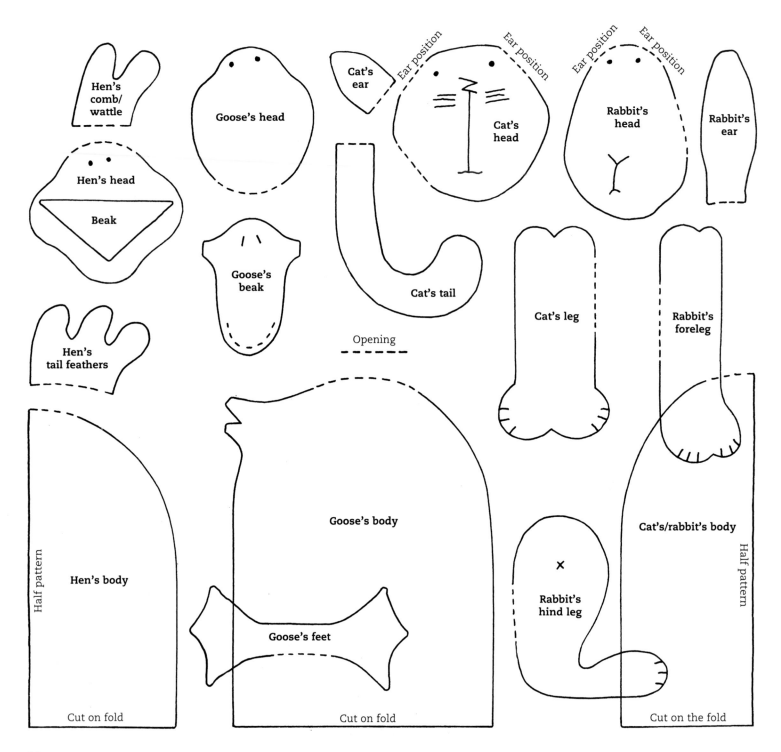

Hen's comb/wattle

Goose's head

Cat's ear

Ear position

Ear position

Cat's head

Ear position

Ear position

Rabbit's head

Rabbit's ear

Hen's head

Beak

Goose's beak

Cat's tail

Cat's leg

Rabbit's foreleg

Hen's tail feathers

Opening

Hen's body

Half pattern

Goose's body

Cat's/rabbit's body

Half pattern

Goose's feet

Rabbit's hind leg

×

Cut on fold

Cut on fold

Cut on the fold

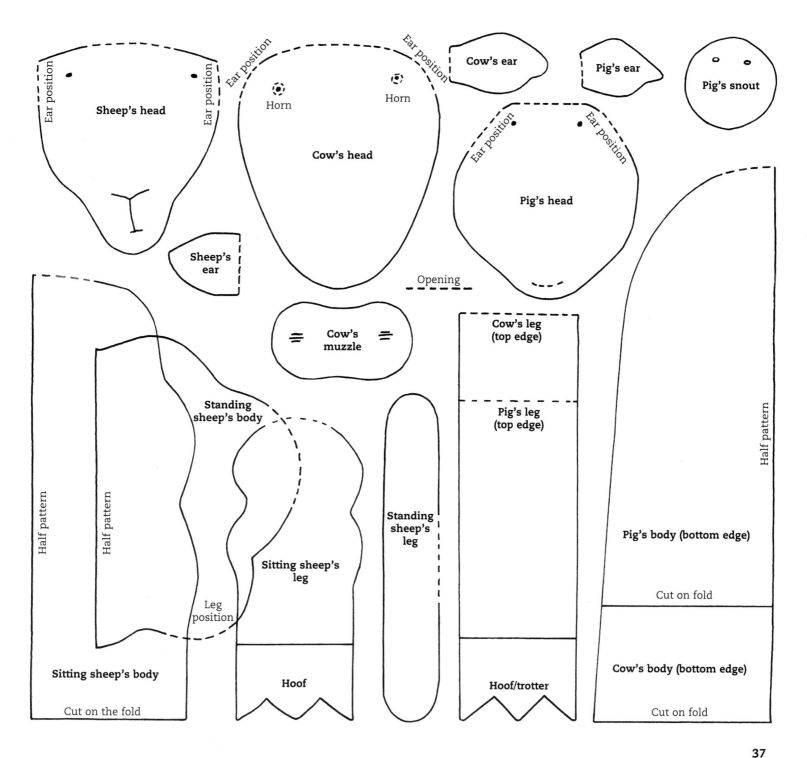

Sheep's head

Ear position

Ear position

Cow's head

Horn

Horn

Ear position

Ear position

Cow's ear

Pig's ear

Pig's snout

Pig's head

Sheep's ear

Opening

Cow's muzzle

Half pattern

Half pattern

Half pattern

Standing sheep's body

Sitting sheep's leg

Standing sheep's leg

Cow's leg (top edge)

Pig's leg (top edge)

Pig's body (bottom edge)

Cut on fold

Half pattern

Leg position

Sitting sheep's body

Hoof

Cut on the fold

Hoof/trotter

Cow's body (bottom edge)

Cut on fold

Noah's Ark Cushion

This clever cushion has a handy front pocket that marks the line between the house and the boat on the Ark. It is an ideal place for small animal couples to cuddle up (see page 31).

The boat can be sewn from thick fabric or from two layers of thinner fabric with wadding in between. The layers are then quilted together on a sewing machine by following the pattern of the fabric or drawn lines.

The cushion is 40 x 40cm (15¾ x 15¾in). For the pattern, see page 41.

Materials for one cushion:
Fabric for the house: 45 x 100cm (17¾ x 39½in)
Fabric for the roof: 15 x 41cm (6 x 16¼in)
Fabric for the boat: 45 x 60cm (17¾ x 23¾in)
Fabric for the gunwale: two pieces each 14 x 41cm (5½ x 16¼in)
Fabric for the label: 6.5 x 13cm (2½ x 5in)
Wadding for the roof: 13 x 41cm (5 x 16¼in)
Fusible wadding for the label: 4.5 x 11.5cm (1¾ x 4½in)
Fabric/bias tape for binding: 6.25 x 85cm (2½ x 33½in)
Three buttons for closing the cushion
Seven buttons for portholes
Four buttons for buttoning on the boat
Cushion pad: 40 x 40cm (15¾ x 15¾in)

1 Draw the pattern full size.
2 Cut two pieces 41 x 69cm (16¼ x 27¼in) and 41 x 29cm (16¼ x 11½in) from the house fabric.
3 Fold 3cm (1¼in) double hems, as shown in figure 1, and sew the hems.
4 Mark and sew three buttons and corresponding buttonholes as shown in figure 1.
5 Button the two pieces together and reinforce the join with stitching at the sides, as shown in figure 2.

6 Fold the seam allowance towards the wrong side on the roof's long edges, open the folds and position the wadding on top.
7 Position the roof in the middle of the house and sew it in place with stitching 2mm (¹⁄₁₆in) from the edges (see figure 2).
8 Fold the fabric wrong sides together, so the short ends are flush and, using the pattern, mark the positions of seven buttons for portholes and two

sets of two buttons to button on the boat. Sew on the buttons (see figure 2).
9 Fold the cushion piece right sides together, so the short ends are flush.
10 Draw the curve of the Ark on the fabric and cut along the drawn line. Sew all round, taking a presser foot's seam allowance (see figure 3).
11 Zigzag the raw edges together and turn the Ark right side out through the button opening (see figure 4).
12 Stuff in the cushion pad.

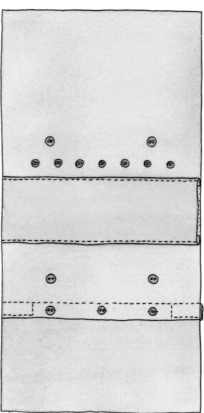

1

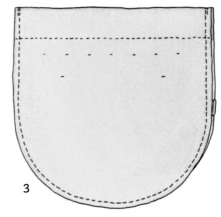

2

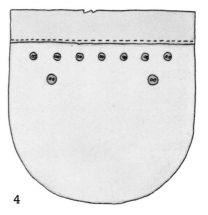

3

4

13 Cut two pieces for the boat, following the pattern.
14 Fold a strip for the gunwale wrong sides together and place it on the wrong side of one boat piece, matching the raw edges. Sew 2cm (¹⁄₁₆in) from the edge (see figure 5a).
15 Fold the strip around the edge to the right side, so it just covers the newly stitched seam, and stitch 2mm (¹⁄₁₆in) from the edge (see figure 5b).
16 Sew the gunwale on the second boat piece in the same way.
17 Sew two buttonholes on each gunwale as marked on the pattern.

18 Draw the text on the label and fuse wadding on to the wrong side.
19 Sew the text using a sewing machine set for a tight zigzag or use embroidery stitches (see figure 6). The stitching lines can be a little staggered – it simply makes the text more alive. Pull the thread ends through to the wrong side and tie them together.
20 Turn under the sides of the label by 1cm (³⁄₈in), position the label on one of the boat pieces and sew it in place.
21 Fold the bias tape in half, wrong sides together.

22 Place the two boat pieces wrong sides together, so the edges are flush, and position the bias tape right sides together with the boat's curved side (see figure 7).
23 Sew on the bias tape, taking a presser foot's seam allowance.
24 Fold the bias tape over to the back of the boat, fold in the ends neatly and sew the tape in place with slipstitches.
25 Button the boat to the house.

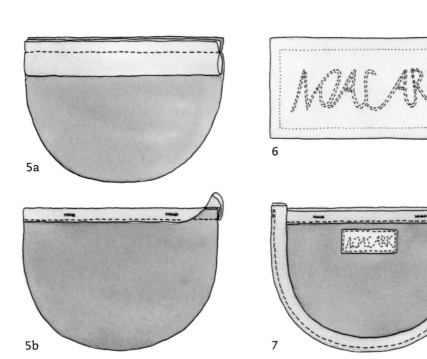

5a

5b

6

7

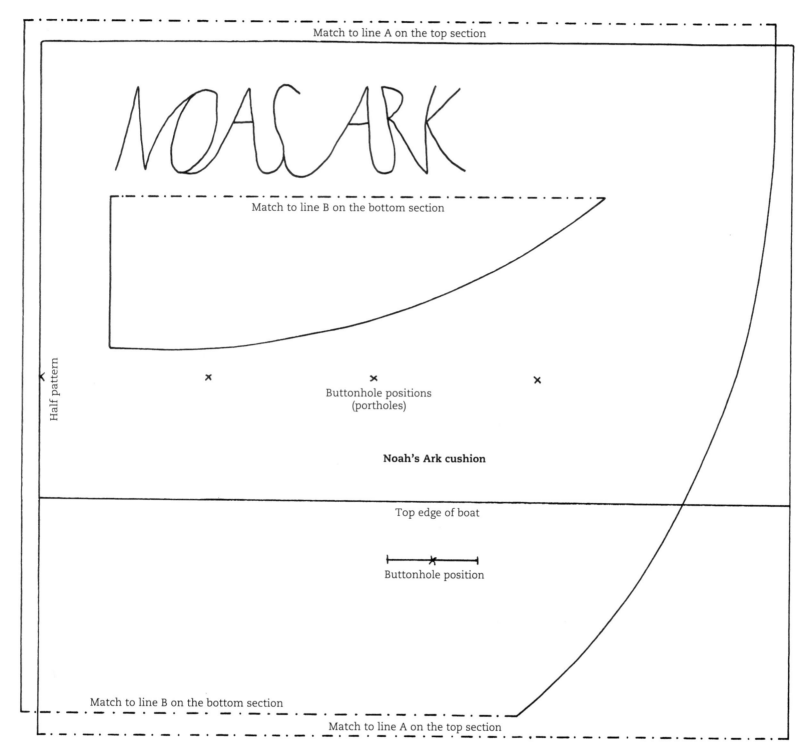

Match to line A on the top section

NOAS ARK

Match to line B on the bottom section

Half pattern

Buttonhole positions
(portholes)

Noah's Ark cushion

Top edge of boat

Buttonhole position

Match to line B on the bottom section

Match to line A on the top section

Coffee Coaster and Placemat

The Ark's shape is practically an open invitation to make a coffee coaster or a placemat. Here, the Ark's dormer becomes a folded strap, which you could use to hang the Ark when not in use.

The pattern on page 26 is for the coffee coaster. For a placemat, the pattern should be enlarged by 250%. This means that one square on the pattern will equal 2.5cm (1in).

Materials for one coffee coaster/ placemat:

Fabric for the roof: 4.5 x 16cm/8 x 38cm (1¾ x 6¼in/3¼ x 15in)

Fabric for the house: 5 x 16cm/ 8.5 x 38cm (2 x 6¼in/3⅜ x 15in)

Fabric for piping: 3 x 16cm/3.5 x 38cm (1¼ x 6¼in/2⅜ x 15in)

Fabric for the boat: 9 x 16cm/22 x 38cm (3½ x 6¼in/8¾ x 15in)

Fabric for the dormer: 8 x 9cm/ 12 x 14cm (3¼ x 3½in/4¾ x 5½in) or see step 5

Fabric for the back: 15.5 x 16cm/ 36 x 38cm (6 x 6¼in/14¼ x 15in)

Wadding: 15.5 x 16cm/36 x 38cm (6 x 6¼in/14¼ x 15in)

Five buttons for the portholes

1 Sew the roof and house strips right sides together, taking a presser foot's seam allowance.

2 Press the seam allowances towards the roof strip.

3 Fold the piping strip wrong sides together. Place the house/roof and the boat fabric right sides together, with the piping in between, and sew, taking a presser foot's seam allowance.

4 Press the seam allowance towards the boat, so the piping naturally lies up over the house (see figure 1).

5 Fold and sew the fabric for the dormer as a folded strap, as explained on page 10. Now fold the strap as shown in figure 2. Alternatively, the dormer for the placemat can be made from two pieces of house fabric 4 x 12cm (1½ x 4¾in) and one piece of roof fabric 10 x 12cm (4 x 4¾in) stitched as shown in figure 3a. Fold, stitch and fold the fabric again as shown in figures 3b–3c.

6 Position the dormer strap in the middle of the roof as shown in figure 4 and sew it in place, taking a presser foot's seam allowance.

7 Place the joined piece right sides together with the fabric for the backing and draw the Ark on top – the pattern should be a seam allowance from the top edge of the roof.

8 Lay the wadding underneath and sew, leaving an opening as shown in figure 5.

9 Cut out, adding a 3mm (⅛in) seam allowance except at the opening where it should be 5mm (¼in). Turn right side out and sew up the opening with slipstitches.

10 Quilt as shown in figure 6 and sew the buttons on as portholes.

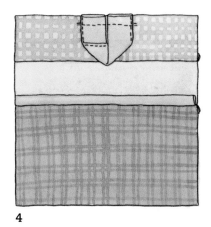

4

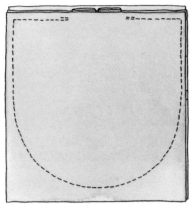

5

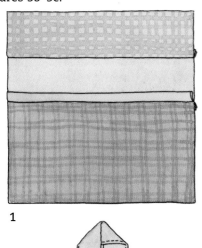

1

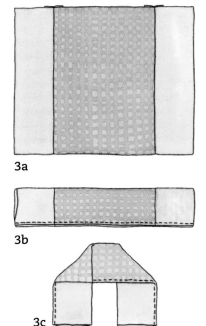

3a

3b

3c

2

6

Cat Cushion

The elongated shape of this cushion is reminiscent of a neck cushion. So now there's no excuse not to relax with a good book. Note that the tail pattern needs to be extended as directed on the pattern, and the opening is at the top.

For the pattern, see page 48.

Materials for one cushion:
Fabric for the body: 53 x 53cm (21 x 21in)
Fabric for the head: 15 x 30cm (6 x 12in)
Fabric for four legs, a tail and two ears: 35 x 40cm (13¾ x 15¾in)
Fabric for a cushion pad: 54 x 54cm (21¼ x 21¼in)
Wadding: 15 x 15cm (6 x 6in)
Zip fastener: 50–55cm (20–22in)
Two buttons for eyes
One button for the tail
Fibrefill

1 Zigzag all edges of the body fabric and sew on the zip as explained on page 10, attaching it to two opposite sides, so the piece takes shape as a tube (see figure 1).

2 Make a head, two ears, four legs and a tail as explained on page 9.

3 Stuff the head moderately with fibrefill, position the ears in the head openings and sew them in place with slipstitches.

4 Sew buttons on as eyes and sew the facial features with long stitches.

5 Stuff the paws firmly and the legs loosely and sew claws as marked on the pattern. Zigzag the raw edges of the opening together on each leg.

6 Stuff the tip of the tail moderately, and the remainder so that the tail is flexible. Fold the seam allowances to the wrong side at the opening and sew with slipstitches.

7 Turn the body tube wrong side out and fold it so that the zip is 3cm (1¼in) from the bottom fold. Open the zip halfway so you can turn the body out later.

8 Position the legs right sides together with the body, with raw edges matching at the side seams. Sew the seams, taking a presser foot's seam allowance (see figure 1).

9 Turn the body right side out and appliqué the head in place.

10 Attach the tail to the body with a button (see figure 2).

11 Make a cushion pad as explained on page 10, and stuff it in the cat's body.

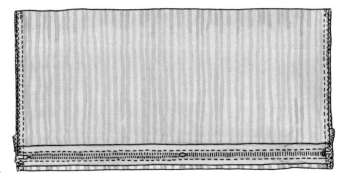

1

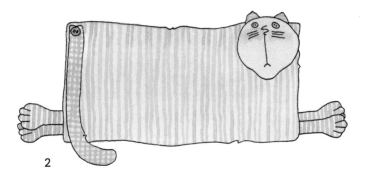

2

Sheep Cushion

The sheep, which doubles as a nice cuddly toy, is super soft when made in towelling or acrylic fleece. The sheep measures 40 x 40cm (16 x 16in). For the pattern, see page 49.

Materials for one cushion:
Fabric for the head: 18.5 x 34cm (7¼ x 13½in)
Fabric for the ears: 7.5 x 26cm (3 x 6¼in)
Fabric for the legs: 7 x 60cm (2¾ x 23¾in)
Fabric for the hooves: 7 x 60cm (2¾ x 23¾in)
Towelling or acrylic fleece for the body: 41 x 83cm (16¼ x 32¾in)
Fusible wadding for the head: 17 x 18.5cm (6¾ x 7¼in)
Fusible wadding for the ears: 7.5 x 13cm (3 x 5in)
Two buttons for eyes
Fibrefill
Zip fastener: 40cm (16in)
Cushion pad: 40 x 40cm (16 x 16in)

1 Fold the fabric pieces for the head and ears right sides together and iron the fusible wadding to the back.

2 Make a head and two ears as explained on page 9. This time you are not going to stuff with fibrefill. Add buttons for eyes and work the nose and mouth with backstitch.

3 Fold the ears to fit in the head openings and sew in place with slipstitches.

4 Sew the leg and hoof strips right sides together. Press the seam allowances towards the hoof fabric and topstitch it in place.

5 Cut out and make four legs as explained on page 9. Turn them right side out.

6 Stuff the legs with fibrefill and zigzag the raw edges of the opening together.

7 Cut one piece of towelling/fleece 41 x 61cm (16¼ x 24in) and one piece 41 x 22cm (16¼ x 8¾in). Zigzag all the raw edges of each piece.

8 Sew the zip right sides together with the two pieces as explained on page 10 (see figure 1).

9 Fold the piece wrong sides together to see where to position the head, then unfold and appliqué the sheep's head on the front, as shown in figure 2. Position the legs right sides together with the body also.

10 Open the zip halfway, fold the body right sides together and sew the three open sides of the cushion (being careful not to catch the ear in the seam).

11 Turn right side out through the zip and stuff the cushion pad inside.

46

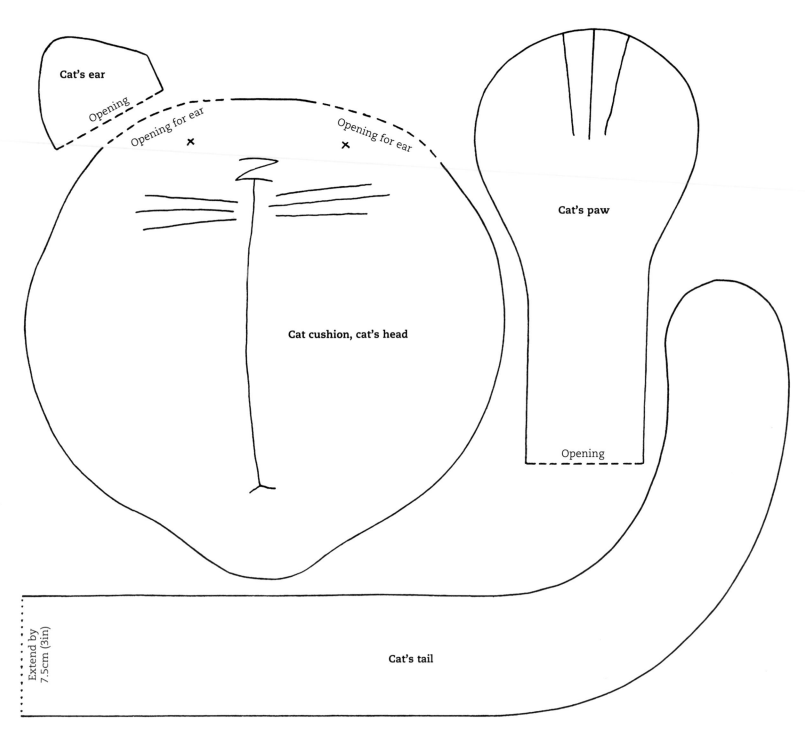

Cat's ear

Opening

Opening for ear

Opening for ear

Cat's paw

Cat cushion, cat's head

Opening

Extend by
7.5cm (3in)

Cat's tail

48

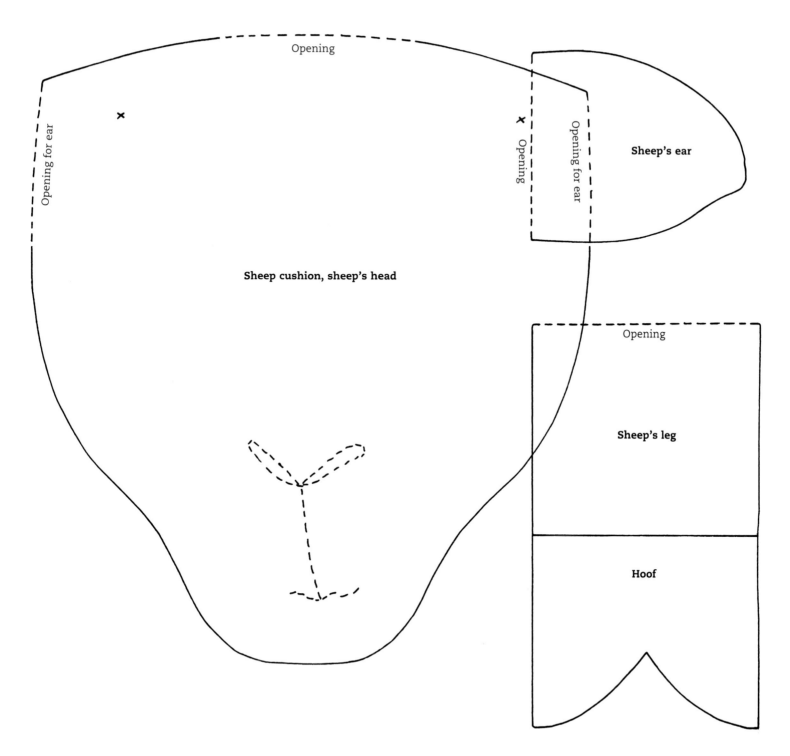

Opening

Opening for ear

×

Sheep cushion, sheep's head

Sheep's ear

Opening for ear

×

Opening

Opening

Sheep's leg

Hoof

Door Duck

This door duck is 24 x 30cm (9½ x 12in) and contains a hidden bag of sand so it can be used as a doorstop. If the duck is intended to hold a large, heavy door, it must be enlarged and the filling increased. The duck can also be put outside with a sign saying 'welcome', 'gone to lunch' or 'back in a moment', for example.

The beak, tail feathers and feet are sewn from fabric remnants.

For the pattern, see page 54.

Materials:

Fabric and fusible wadding remnants
  for the beak, tail feathers and feet
Fabric for the head: 13 x 23cm (5 x 9in)
Fabric for the wings: 15 x 40cm
  (6 x 16in)
Fabric for the strap: 10 x 20cm (4 x 8in)
Fabric for the body: 25 x 85cm
  (10 x 33½in)
Fabric for the weight bag: 25 x 85cm
  (10 x 33½in)
Fusible wadding: 15 x 35cm (6 x 13¾in)
Fusible interfacing: 23 x 28cm (9 x 11in)
Two small buttons for eyes
Five buttons for wings and closure
Fibrefill
Clean, dry sand or similar
  heavy material

1 Draw the patterns full size.

2 Fold the fabric for one beak, three tail feathers, two feet, a head and two wings right sides together and draw the appropriate patterns on top.

3 Iron the wadding on to the back of the fabrics and sew the pieces as explained on page 9.

4 Stuff the head and beak with fibrefill and sew up the openings with slipstitches.

5 Appliqué the beak to the head then embroider the nasal openings and add a smile on the beak with running stitches.

6 Sew on buttons as eyes.

7 Sew up the openings on the wings with slipstitches and quilt the wings, tail feathers and feet on the sewing machine about a presser foot's width in.

8 Stuff a little fibrefill in the tail feathers and in the feet within the quilt line.

9 Fold and sew the strap as explained on page 10.

10 Cut one back piece and two front pieces using the pattern on page 54 – the upper body section should be extended by 9cm (3½in) and the lower body section by 6cm (2¼in) as indicated on the pattern.

11 Stitch a 3cm (1¼in) double hem on each front piece, as shown in figure 1. Mark and sew three buttonholes on the top front piece and three buttons on the bottom front piece as shown in figure 1. Button the fronts together.

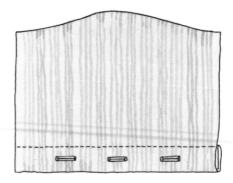
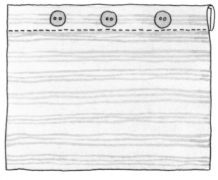

1

12 Position the strap and the tail feathers right sides together with the buttoned-up front piece.

13 Place the back piece right sides together with the front and sew the top and both sides, taking a presser foot's seam allowance, as shown in figure 2.

14 Zigzag the raw edges together.

15 Position the feet between the front and back pieces.

16 Fold 2.5cm (1in) pleats at the sides as shown in figure 3 and sew the bottom seam, taking a presser foot's seam allowance. Zigzag the raw edges together.

17 Turn out the body, position the head and appliqué it in place.

18 Position the wings and sew them in place with buttons.

19 There are two weight/filling bags. Cut a piece of fabric 23 x 55cm (9 x 21¾in) for the top one, fold it right sides together and draw around the pattern for the body (see figure 4). Sew as shown, leaving an opening in one side seam. Trim the seam allowance at the top of the bag.

20 Fold pleats at the bottom of the bag as on the duck's body and sew in place.

21 Cut two pieces of fabric each 14 x 23cm (5½ x 9in) for the bottom weight bag. It is a good idea to iron fusible interfacing to the wrong side to seal the fabric.

22 Sew the fabric pieces together with right sides facing, leaving an opening in one side seam as shown in figure 5.

23 Fold pleats in the sides at both the top and the bottom and sew in place.

24 Turn out both weight bags. Stuff the upper bag firmly with fibrefill and the lower one with dry sand or a similar heavy material.

25 Put the stuffed bags in the duck's body and button up.

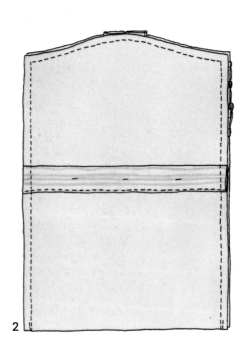

2

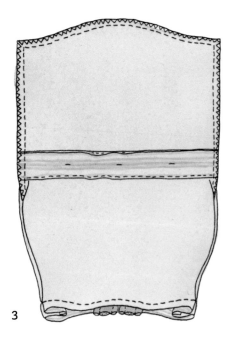

3

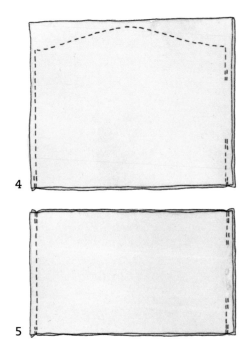

4

5

1

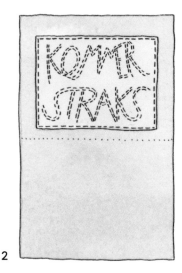

2

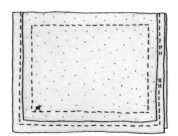

3

Signs

Many different things can be written on the duck's signs, which are sewn in two sizes. The text used here is on page 55.

Materials for both signs:
Fabric for the text: 12 x 15cm/
11 x 20cm (4¾ x 6in/4¼ x 8in)
Fabric for the backing: 17 x 26cm/
21.5 x 24.5cm (6¾ x 10¼in/8½ x 9¾in)
Fusible wadding for the text:
10 x 13cm/9 x 18cm (4 x 5in/3½ x 7in)
Fusible wadding for the backing:
12 x 15cm/11.5 x 20cm (4¾ x 6in/
4½ x 8in)
Two buttons per sign
String: 30cm (12in) per sign

1 Write the text on the fabric and iron the wadding centrally on the wrong side.
2 Sew the text with tight zigzag stitches on a sewing machine or with appropriate embroidery stitches.
3 Pull the top thread ends through to the underside and tie the threads together; trim the ends.
4 Fold a seam allowance to the wrong side along the sides of the sign and tack if desired.
5 Fold the backing fabric right sides together and iron the wadding on to the wrong side, so it follows the fold (see figure 1).
6 Open the fabric and centre the text sign on the right side over the wadding, 1cm (⅜in) from the fold. Sew it in place 2mm (¹⁄₁₆in) from the edge (see figure 2).
7 Fold the backing fabric again and sew along the three open sides, leaving an opening (see figure 3).
8 Turn right side out and sew up the opening with slipstitches.
9 Sew two buttons on the sign and twist the string around them. The sign can now be hung on one of the duck's wings.

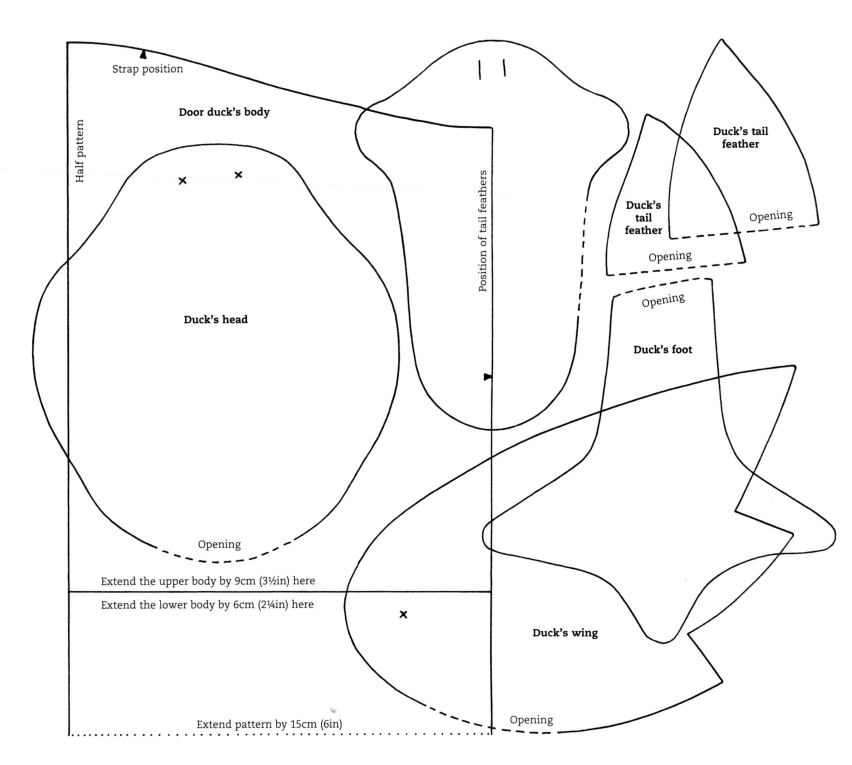

Strap position

Half pattern

Door duck's body

Position of tail feathers

Duck's tail feather

Duck's tail feather

Opening

Opening

Opening

Duck's head

✗ ✗

Duck's foot

Opening

Opening

Extend the upper body by 9cm (3½in) here

Extend the lower body by 6cm (2¼in) here

✗

Duck's wing

Extend pattern by 15cm (6in)

Opening

54

KOMMER
STRAKS
ER I HAVEN
⟶

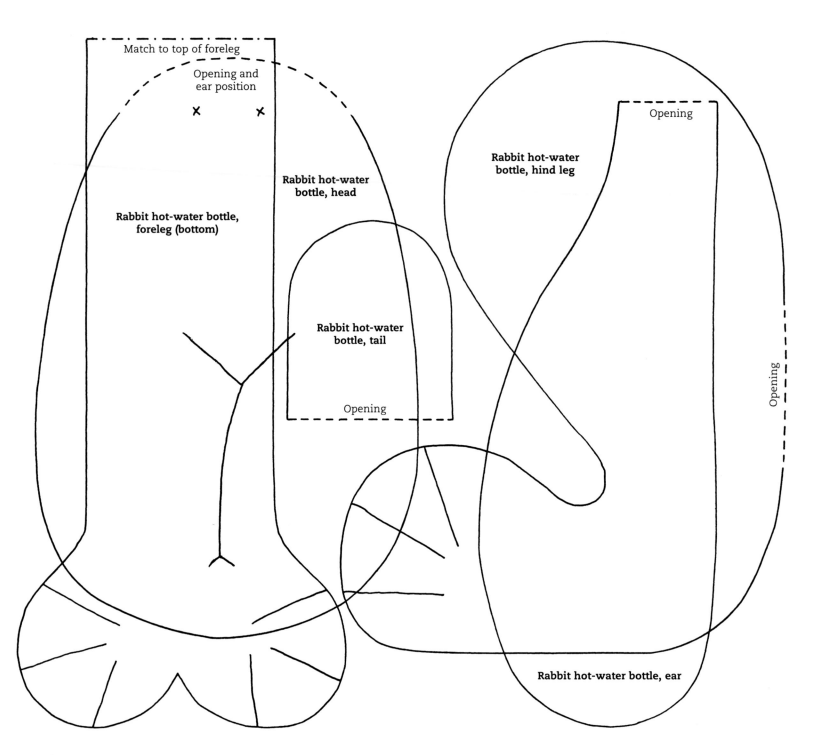

Match to top of foreleg

Opening and ear position

✗ ✗

Rabbit hot-water bottle, foreleg (bottom)

Rabbit hot-water bottle, head

Rabbit hot-water bottle, tail

Opening

Rabbit hot-water bottle, hind leg

Opening

Opening

Rabbit hot-water bottle, ear

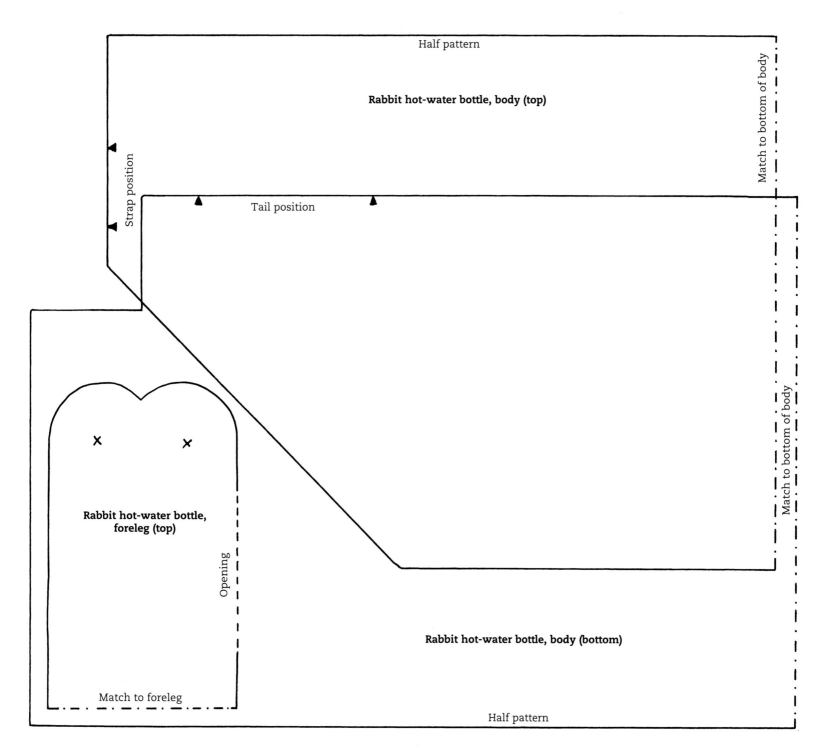

Half pattern

Rabbit hot-water bottle, body (top)

Match to bottom of body

Strap position

Tail position

Rabbit hot-water bottle, foreleg (top)

Opening

Match to bottom of body

Match to foreleg

Rabbit hot-water bottle, body (bottom)

Half pattern

Rabbit Hot-water Bottle Cover

This cuddly rabbit is roughly 27 x 40cm (10½ x 16in), so there is room for a traditional hot-water bottle. The body is lined to cover the seams and is closed at the bottom with a zip. The rabbit is made in towelling, but acrylic fleece or synthetic fur fabric is fine too – they are soft against cold feet. For the pattern, see pages 56–57.

Materials for one rabbit:
Towelling for the head, legs and tail: 35 x 50cm (13¾ x 19¾in)
Towelling for the ears: 20 x 20cm (8 x 8in)
Towelling for the body: 30 x 80cm (12 x 31½in)
Fabric for the ears: 20 x 20cm (8 x 8in)
Fabric for strap: 8 x 20cm (3 x 8in)
Fabric for lining: 30 x 80cm (12 x 31½in)
Fibrefill
Two small buttons for eyes
Two large buttons for the legs
Zip fastener: 25cm (10in)

1 Draw the patterns full size.
2 Fold the towelling for one head, one foreleg, one hind leg and one tail and sew as explained on page 9.
3 Place the towelling and the fabric for the ears right sides together and sew the ears as explained on page 9 but do not stuff them.
4 Stuff the head well with fibrefill, position the ears in the opening and sew them in place with slipstitches so the opening is also sewn up.
5 Sew small buttons on as eyes and sew the nose and mouth with long stitches.
6 Stuff fibrefill in the tail and the front and hind paws, and sew the paws as marked on the pattern.

7 Sew up the openings on the legs with slipstitches.
8 Fold and stitch a strap as explained on page 10.
9 Cut two towelling bodies and two lining bodies.
10 Place a towelling body right sides together with a lining body and place the zip in between with the right side against the towelling.
11 Sew in place, taking a presser foot's seam allowance (see figure 1).
12 Open out the pieces just stitched so that the body pieces are wrong sides together and topstitch along the zip (see figure 2).
13 Sew the other towelling and lining body pieces to the zip's other side in the same way.

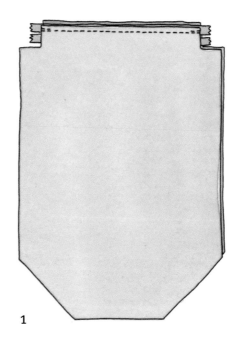

1

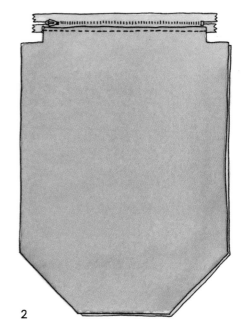

2

14 Position the forelegs and hind leg on the right side of one of the towelling bodies, 4.5cm (1¾in) from the zip and 3.5cm (1½in) from the side seams; turn the other layers away.
15 Sew the forelegs in place with stitching in the middle and sew the buttons on top.
16 Appliqué the hind leg in place.
17 Place the towelling body and the lining body right sides together separately.
18 Place the strap and the tail between the parts of the towelling body as marked on the pattern.

19 Sew the towelling body's side seams and 'neck' and the lining body's side seams, taking a presser foot's seam allowance (see figure 3).
20 Open the zip halfway, place one seam of the towelling body right sides together with the zip and place one side seam of the lining body right sides together with the zip's back side. Sew through all the layers as shown in the figure 4.
21 Sew the other corner in the same way.

22 Place the towelling body and the lining body wrong sides together and sew the shoulder seams (see figure 5).
23 Turn right side out through the 'neck' of the lining body and sew up the opening with slipstitches.
24 Appliqué the head on to the body.

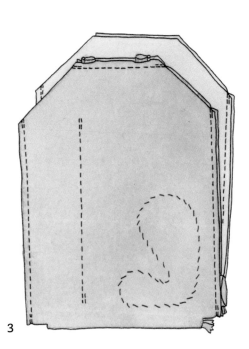

3

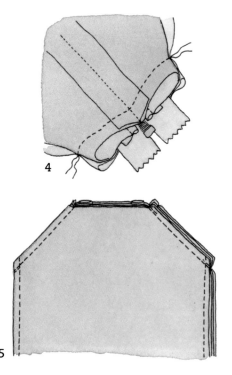

4

5

Playful Pigs

These charming pigs turn up in summer clothes and with lifebuoys, ready for a summer cruise. They are approximately 42cm (16¼in) tall. For the pattern, see page 66.

Materials for one pig:
Skin-coloured fabric for the body: 45 x 55cm (17¾ x 21¾in)
Fabric for trotters: 6 x 46cm (2⅜ x 18in)
Fusible wadding: 15 x 17cm (6 x 6¾in)
Fibrefill

1 Draw the pattern full size.
2 Cut pieces from the skin-coloured fabric 17 x 46cm (6¾ x 18in) for the arms/legs, 25 x 27cm (10 x 10¾in) for the body, 12 x 27cm (4¾ x 10¾in) for the head, 5 x 11cm (2 x 4¼in) for the snout and 5 x 20cm (2 x 8in) for the ears.
3 Sew the fabric for the arms/legs right sides together with the fabric for the trotters. Press the seam allowances on to the trotter fabric and topstitch them in place.
4 Fold and sew the pieces for the head and the snout right sides together, as shown in figure 1a, leaving central openings. Press the seam allowances open.
5 Iron wadding on to the back of each joined piece and sew the head and snout as shown in figure 1b.
6 Fold the fabric for the ears right sides together and iron wadding on to the back.

7 Fold the fabric for the arms/legs and the fabric for the body right sides together and sew two ears, two arms, two legs and a body as explained on page 9. The legs and the body must have openings at the top and bottom respectively.
8 Stuff a little fibrefill into the ears and snout and quilt 2mm (1/16in) from the edge.
9 Sew nostrils on the snout with backstitches or French knots and sew up the opening with slipstitches.
10 Position the ears in the head, sew them in place with slipstitches and stuff the head very firmly.
11 Appliqué on the nose, sew the eyes with French knots and sew the mouth with backstitches.
12 Stuff the arms and legs with fibrefill firmly halfway up and loosely thereafter.
13 Sew up the openings of the arms with slipstitches.
14 Position the legs right sides together with the front of the body and sew them in place, taking a presser foot's seam all around the bottom of the body – this provides a marker that the seam allowance can be folded along.
15 Stuff the body firmly with fibrefill, being extra careful at the neck. Tuck in the seam allowances at the bottom of the body and sew up the opening with slipstitches. Do not sew on the head until the T-shirt/dress is pulled on to the body (see pages 62 and 64).

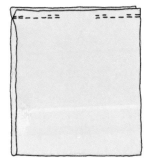

1a

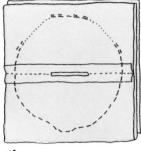

1b

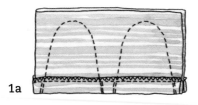

1a

1b

2a

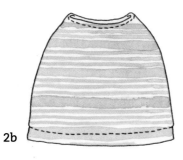

2b

T-shirt

For the pattern, see page 67.

Materials:

Fabric: 30 x 38cm (12 x 15in)
Two buttons for the arms

1 Cut a piece of fabric 9.5 x 30cm (3¾ x 12in) for the sleeves.
2 Zigzag one of the long edges, press a 1.5cm (⅝in) hem towards the wrong side and sew in place.
3 Fold the piece right sides together and sew two sleeves as shown in figure 1a.
4 Cut the sleeves out, adding a 3–4mm (⅛in) seam allowance. Zigzag the raw edges together and turn right side out (see figure 1b).
5 Cut a front and a back piece from the remaining fabric and mark a 1cm (⅜in) hem along the neckline. Cut notches up to the marked line and press the hem towards the wrong side.
6 Sew the hem just inside the folded edge (see figure 2a).

7 Zigzag the T-shirt's bottom edge, press a 1.5cm (⅝in) hem towards the wrong side and sew (see figure 2a).
8 Place the front and back pieces right sides together and sew the side seams, taking a presser foot's seam allowance.
9 Trim the seam allowances back to 3–4mm (⅛in), zigzag the raw edges together and turn right side out (see figure 2b).
10 Put the T-shirt on the body.
11 Put the pig's neck 1.5cm (⅝in) up into the opening on the head and sew the pieces together with slipstitches (see figures 3a and 3b).
12 Put the sleeves on the arms and sew the arms in place on the body with buttons – sew through the body from arm to arm.

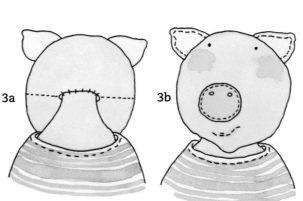

3a   **3b**

Pantalettes and trousers

The pantalettes and the trousers are sewn using the same parts of the pattern and the same method. As marked on the pattern, the trousers are a little longer than the pantalettes. For the pattern, see page 67.

Materials:
Fabric for the pantalettes: 16 x 40cm (6¼ x 16in)
Fabric for the trousers: 21 x 40cm (8¼ x 16in)
1cm (⅜in) elastic: 25cm (10in)

1 Draw the pattern full size.
2 Cut two pantalette or trouser legs on the fold and place them right sides together (see figure 1a).
3 Sew the centre-front (CF) seam, taking a presser foot's seam allowance, and then zigzag the raw edges together. Also zigzag the top and bottom edges as shown.
4 Fold and press a 1.5cm (⅝in) hem towards the wrong side at the waist and bottom edges as shown in figure 1b and sew the bottom hems only.
5 Open the hem along the top edge and sew the centre-back (CB) seam in the same way as the centre front.
6 Refold and sew the top hem, leaving a small opening to thread the elastic through.
7 Place the centre-front and centre-back seams together with right sides facing and sew the inside-leg seams. Zigzag the raw edges together.

8 Thread the elastic into the drawstring hem and sew the ends together with small overcast stitches.

Summer dress

Materials:
Fabric: 40 x 50cm (16 x 19¾in)
Two buttons for the arms

1 Cut pieces 9.5 x 30cm (3¾ x 12in) for the sleeves, 13 x 34cm (5 x 13½in) for the bodice and 13.5 x 50cm (5¼ x 19¾in) for the skirt.
2 Sew the sleeves and bodice as for the T-shirt (see page 62) but do not hem the lower edge of the bodice.
3 Press 1.5cm (⅝in) towards the wrong side on one long edge of the skirt (bottom edge) and open the fold again.
4 Zigzag along all the raw edges of the skirt, fold the piece right sides together and sew the short ends together, taking a presser foot's seam allowance (see figure 2a). Press the seam allowances open.
5 Refold and sew the bottom hem as shown in figure 2b.
6 Sew gathering threads along the upper edge of the skirt.
7 Pin the bodice right sides together with the skirt as shown in figure 2b, gather the skirt to fit and sew together, taking a presser foot's seam allowance.
8 Remove the gathering threads.
9 Put the dress on the body and sew the head in place as described on page 62 and illustrated there in figures 3a and 3b.
10 Put the sleeves on the arms and attach the arms to the body with buttons – sew through the body from arm to arm.

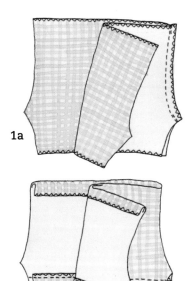

1a

1b

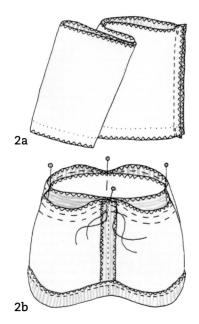

2a

2b

Lifebuoy

Materials for one buoy:
Fabric for the lifebuoy: 11 x 45cm
(4¼ x 17¾in), cut on the bias
Fabric for the marking band:
7.5 x 50cm (3 x 19¾in)
Fusible wadding: 9 x 43cm (3½ x 17in)
5mm (¼in) tape for the 'grab line',
55cm (21¾in) long
Fibrefill

1 Iron the wadding centrally on to the wrong side of the lifebuoy strip (see figure 1).
2 Fold the strip right sides together and sew as shown in figure 2 – start and stop the stitching 5cm (2in) from the short ends.
3 Turn the piece right side out, place the short ends right sides together and sew as shown in figure 3.
4 Stuff the buoy firmly with fibrefill and sew up the opening with slipstitches.
5 Fold and sew the marking band as shown in figure 2 – here, however, sew right to the ends and do not use wadding.
6 Turn the band right side out and press it with the seam centred. Topstitch the edges.
7 Cut four pieces from the band, each 12cm (4¾in).
8 Sew the short ends of the grab-line tape together with small stitches and wrap it around the buoy. Hold the line in place with pins.
9 Wrap each of the four marking bands around the buoy, fold a hem on one short end and sew over the other end with slipstitches (see figure 4). Remove the pins holding the grab line.

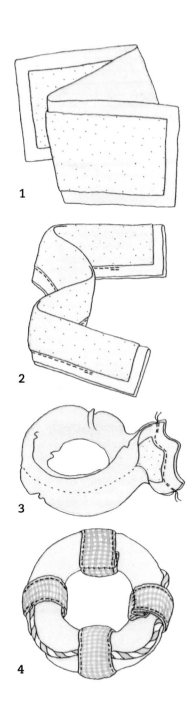

1

2

3

4

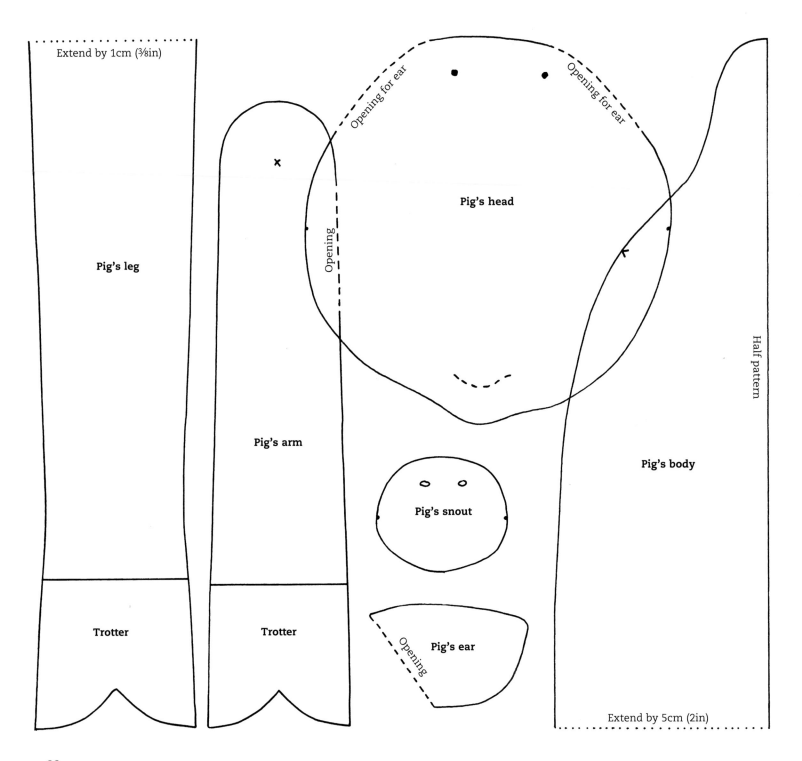

Extend by 1cm (⅜in)

Pig's leg

Trotter

Pig's arm

Opening

Trotter

Opening for ear

Pig's head

Opening for ear

Pig's snout

Pig's ear

Opening

Half pattern

Pig's body

Extend by 5cm (2in)

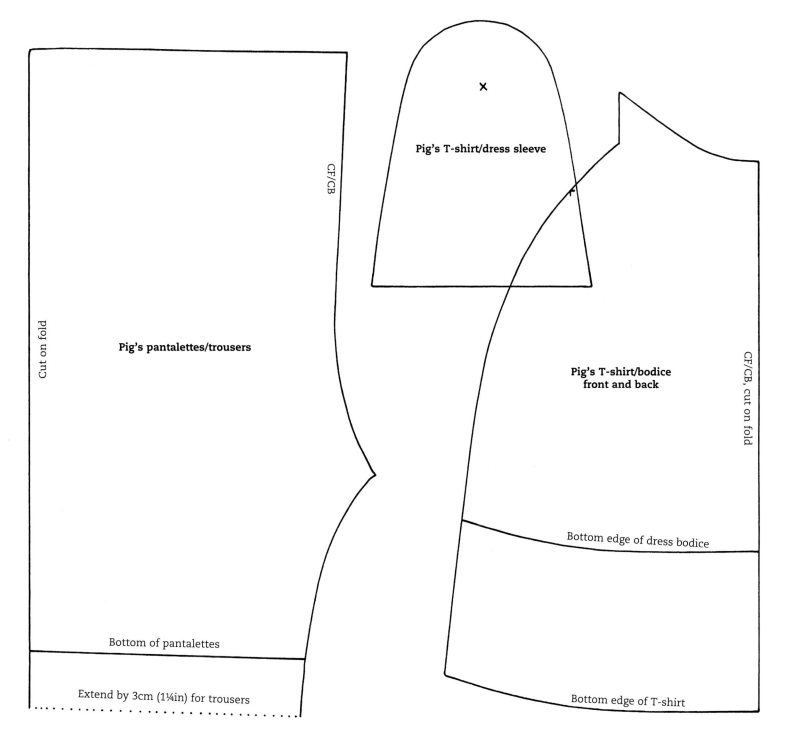

Cut on fold

CF/CB

Pig's pantalettes/trousers

Pig's T-shirt/dress sleeve

X

Pig's T-shirt/bodice front and back

CF/CB, cut on fold

Bottom edge of dress bodice

Bottom of pantalettes

Extend by 3cm (1¼in) for trousers

Bottom edge of T-shirt

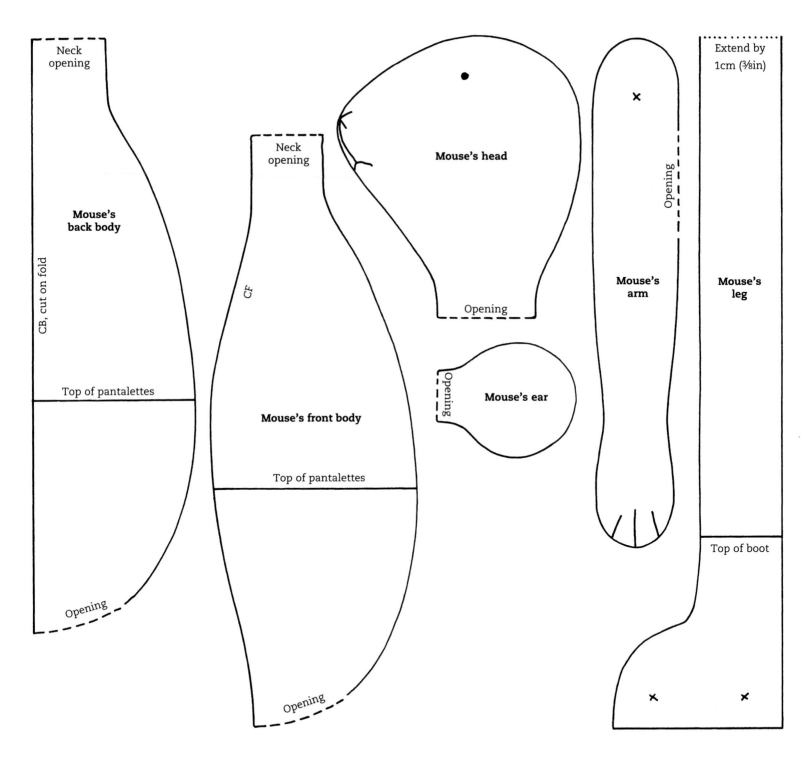

Neck opening

Mouse's back body

CB, cut on fold

Top of pantalettes

Opening

Neck opening

CF

Mouse's front body

Top of pantalettes

Opening

Mouse's head

Opening

Opening

Mouse's ear

Opening

Mouse's arm

Extend by 1cm (⅜in)

Mouse's leg

Top of boot

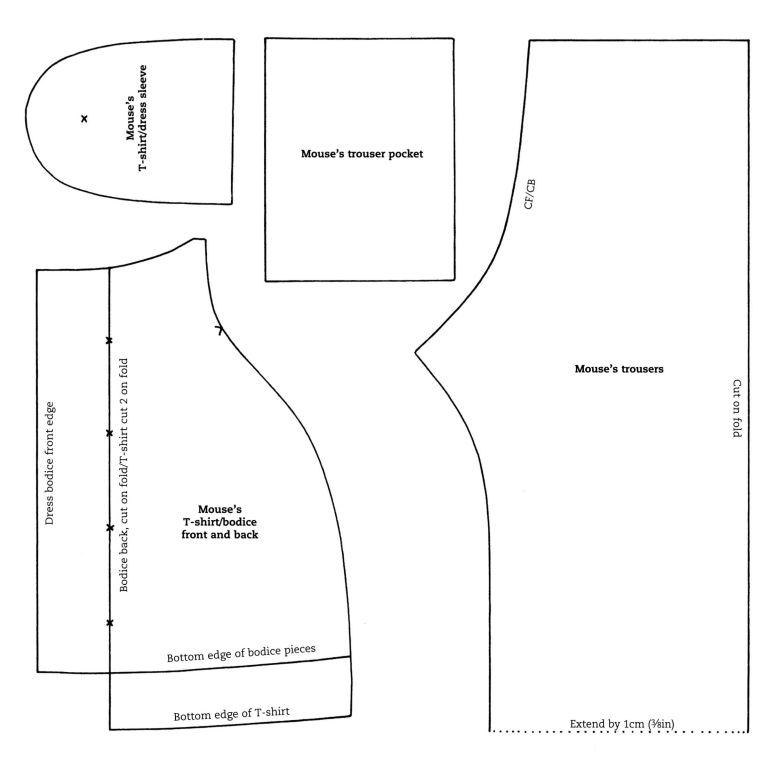

Mouse's
T-shirt/dress sleeve

Mouse's trouser pocket

CF/CB

Mouse's trousers

Cut on fold

Dress bodice front edge

Bodice back, cut on fold/T-shirt cut 2 on fold

Mouse's
T-shirt/bodice
front and back

Bottom edge of bodice pieces

Bottom edge of T-shirt

Extend by 1cm (⅜in)

69

Roller-skating Mice

These sporty mice have strapped on roller skates, so they are ready to roll on board the Ark. Both mice are basically sewn in the same way, but the girl is wearing pantalettes – the top part forms the lower part of the body while the legs of the pantalettes are separate.

If the body is stuffed really firmly, each mouse can keep its balance on its own. The mice are approximately 36cm (14in) tall.

For the pattern, see page 68.

Materials for one mouse:
Fabric for the body: 35 x 60cm (13¾ x 23½in)
Fabric for the pantalettes: 8 x 50cm (3¼ x 19¾in)
Fabric for the boots: 7 x 25cm (2¾ x 10in)
Fibrefill
Old brush or twine for the whiskers
Eight buttons for wheels

1 Draw the pattern for the leg full size and mark an opening at the top.
2 Cut a rectangle of body fabric 15 x 30cm (6 x 12in) for one head, two ears and two arms.
3 Cut a piece of body fabric 16 x 25cm (6¼ x 10in) and sew it right sides together with the boot fabric, taking a presser foot's seam allowance.

4 Press the seam allowances towards the boot fabric and topstitch them in place.
5 Fold the fabrics right sides together and sew the pieces as explained on page 9.
6 Mark the neck seam allowance with tacking stitches and stuff the head firmly with fibrefill.
7 Tuck in the seam allowances at the openings on the ears and sew them up with slipstitches.
8 Position the ears on the head and slipstitch in place.
9 Sew the eyes with French knots and the nose and mouth with backstitches.
10 Sew the whiskers, which can be cut from a brush or rough twine, for example, in place under the nose (see figure 1).
11 Stuff the arms firmly with fibrefill approximately halfway up and loosely after that.
12 Sew up the openings of the arms with slipstitches.
13 Sew 'fingers' with backstitches as marked on the pattern. Put the arms aside for later – they are sewn on to the body at the same time as the sleeves of the dress or T-shirt.
14 Stuff the legs very firmly with fibrefill, right up to the top.
15 Sew four buttons on each boot as wheels.

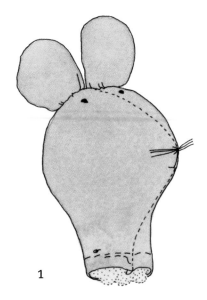

1

16 For the girl mouse, cut a piece of body fabric 11 x 26cm (4¼ x 10¼in) and a piece of pantalette fabric 8 x 26cm (3¼ x 10¼in). Sew the pieces right sides together, press the seam allowances towards the pantalette fabric and topstitch them in place.
Alternatively, for the boy mouse, cut a piece of body fabric 16 x 26cm (6¼ x 10¼in).
17 For both mice, cut a back body piece from the fabric as shown in figure 2.
18 Fold the remaining fabric right sides together, mark the front body piece on top and then sew the centre-front (CF) seam as shown in figure 3.

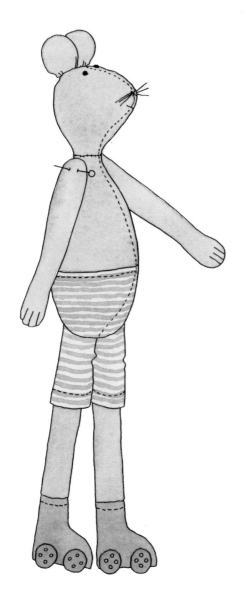

19 Trim the centre-front seam allowances back to 3mm (⅛in). Cut out the front body and open it out.

20 Mark the seam allowances with tacking thread at the neck and the opening.

21 Place the back and the front body right sides together and stitch the sides, taking a presser foot's seam allowance, as shown in figure 4.

22 Trim the side-seam allowances back to 3mm (⅛in).

23 Turn the body right side out and stuff it very firmly.

24 For the girl mouse only, cut a piece of fabric 8 x 16cm (3¼ x 6¼in) for the pantalette legs. Zigzag one long edge then fold 1.5cm (⅝in) to the wrong side and sew the hem.

25 Fold the fabric as shown in figure 5 and sew the inside-leg seams, taking a presser foot's seam allowance.

26 Cut the legs apart and zigzag the raw edges together.

27 Turn the legs right side out and put them on the girl mouse's legs.

28 For both mice, tuck the seam allowance on the body's opening inside, position the legs and sew them in place with slipstitches.

29 For the girl mouse only, tuck the seam allowance at the neck of the body inside and sew the head in place with slipstitches. (The boy mouse's head is not attached until he is wearing his T-shirt.)

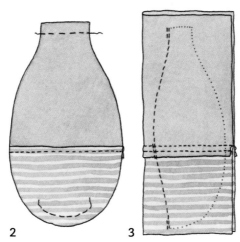

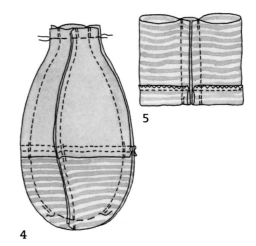

2   3   4   5

T-shirt

For the pattern, see page 69.

Materials:
Fabric: 23 x 30cm (9 x 12in)
Two buttons for the arms

1 Cut an 8 x 24cm (3¼ x 9½in) piece of fabric for the sleeves and sew the T-shirt as explained on page 62 for the pig.
2 Put the T-shirt on the body and sew the boy mouse's head in place with slipstitches.
3 Put the sleeves on the arms and sew them on to the body with buttons – sew through the body from arm to arm.

Trousers

For the pattern, see page 69.

Materials:

Fabric: 20 x 55cm (8 x 21¾in)
1cm (⅜in) elastic: 20cm (8in)

1 Cut a 14cm (5½in) square of fabric for two pockets.
2 Fold the fabric right sides together and sew the pockets as shown in figure 1a.
3 Cut out the pockets, adding a 3mm (⅛in) seam allowance to the sides and turn right side out.

4 Topstitch 7.5mm (a generous ¼in) from the edges as shown in figure 1b. Work an extra line of topstitching along the top edge.
5 Cut two trouser legs from the remaining fabric.
6 Position the pockets 3cm (1¼in) in from the sides of the legs and 3.5cm (1⅜in) up from the bottom edge (see figure 2).
7 Sew the pockets in place just inside the edge.
8 Sew the trousers as explained on page 64 but work two rows of stitching on the outside leg and hem edges (see figure 3).

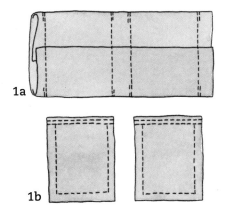

1a

1b

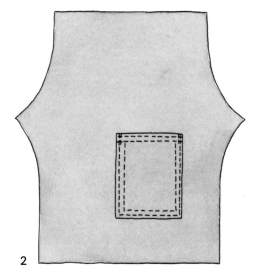

2

3

Dress

For the pattern, see page 69.

Materials:

Fabric: 30 x 40cm (12 x 16in)
Four small buttons for the front
Two buttons for the arms

1 Cut a piece of fabric 10 x 40cm (4 x 16in) for the skirt and a piece 8 x 24cm (3¼ x 9½in) for the sleeves.
2 Cut a back piece and two front pieces for the bodice of the dress.
3 Mark a 7.5mm (generous ¼in) hem along the neckline, cut small notches up to the marked line and press the hem towards the wrong side.
4 Sew the hems 2mm (¹⁄₁₆in) from the edge (see figure 1).
5 Zigzag along the front edges of the front pieces and fold 1.5cm (⅝in) over to the wrong side.

6 Mark the position of four buttons and sew on the two lowest buttons through both front pieces (see figure 2).
7 Place the front pieces right sides together with the back piece and sew the side seams, taking a presser foot's seam allowance. Trim the seam allowance back to 3mm (⅛in) and zigzag the raw edges together.
8 Zigzag the lower edge of the bodice and turn right side out.
9 Sew the sleeves for the dress as explained on page 62.
10 Make the skirt and stitch it to the bodice as explained on page 64.
11 Put the dress on the body and sew on the two top buttons through both front pieces.
12 Put the sleeves on the arms and sew them on to the body with buttons – sew through the body from arm to arm.

1

2

Fabulous Fish

This section is totally fishy – fortunately in a good way! There are fish to take hold of hot items, but also fish you can take with you into town – in the form of a smart herring clutch bag and matching make-up bag. The fishes' eyes are buttons, and you can create a fish-eye effect if two buttons are sewn together, with a small button on top of a larger one.

Pan herring

This herring is not going in the pan, but around the handle. It is lined with insulated wadding, so you will not burn yourself when a hot pan has to be moved. The herring is 8 x 23cm (3¼ x 9in).
For the pattern, see page 81.

Materials for one herring:
Fabric for the body: 22 x 50cm (8¾ x 19½in)
Fabric for the head: 8 x 15cm (3¼ x 6in)
Fabric for the fins: 9 x 17cm (3½ x 6¾in)
Fabric for the strap: 4 x 9cm (1½ x 3½in)
Insulated wadding: 22 x 25cm (8¾ x 9¾in)
Fusible wadding: 4.5 x 17cm (1¾ x 6¾in)
Four buttons for eyes: a small pair and a larger pair

1 Draw the pattern for the body full size.
2 Cut two bodies from the fabric and one from the insulated wadding.
3 Fold the fabric for the fins as shown in figure 1, iron the fusible wadding on to the wrong side and sew two small fins and a tail fin. (The fins can also be sewn from different fabric remnants.)
4 Turn the fins and tail right side out and quilt them on the sewing machine as shown in figure 2.
5 Fold and sew a strap as explained on page 10.
6 Fold and position the strap on the tail fin as shown in figure 3 and sew it in place, taking a presser foot's seam allowance.
7 Fold a seam allowance to the wrong side on the head's straight sides, position the head with its wrong side against the right side of the herring's upper body and put the small fins underneath (see figure 4). Topstitch the head in place just inside the edge.
8 Tack across the opening on both the upper and lower body pieces. Place the upper and lower body right sides together with the insulated wadding under them and sew together, taking a presser foot's seam allowance, as shown in figure 5.
9 Trim the seam allowance back to 3mm (⅛in), except by the opening where it should be 5mm (¼in), and turn right side out.

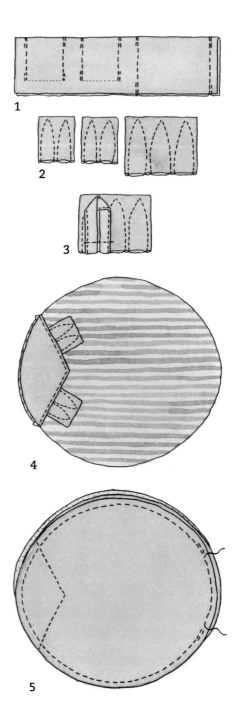

1

2

3

4

5

10 Tuck in the seam allowances at the opening, position the tail fin in the opening and sew it in place with slipstitches.

11 Quilt the herring as shown in figure 6 and sew on buttons as eyes.

12 Fold the herring with the undersides together and sew the bottom 10cm (4in) of the belly together with slipstitches (see the upper folded fish in figure 7).

Plaice potholder/tablemat

Each plaice is lined with insulated wadding, so it can be used as a potholder, just like the herring, or as a tablemat. The plaice, which is closely related to the pan herring from a sewing perspective, is approximately 20cm (8in) in diameter.

For the pattern, see page 81.

Materials for two plaice:

Fabric for the body: 50 x 50cm (19¾ x 19¾in)

Fabric for the head and tail fin: 20 x 30cm (8 x 12in)

Fabric for the fin and strap: 16 x 20cm (6¼ x 8in)

Insulated wadding: 25 x 50cm (9¾ x 19½in)

Fusible wadding: 7 x 32cm (2¾ x 12½in)

Four buttons for eyes: a small pair and a larger pair

1 Make each plaice in the same way. First draw the pattern full size.

2 Cut two bodies from the body fabric and one from insulated wadding.

3 Cut a 6 x 12cm (2⅜ x 4¾in) piece of fabric for the strap and, from the remaining fabric, a head, a small fin and a tail fin.

4 Fold the seam allowance to the wrong side along one curved side of the head.

5 Sew the plaice like the pan herring, but in this case position the strap at the back of the tail fin in the middle (see figure 1).

6 Quilt the plaice as shown in figure 2 – the small fin should be folded to the side when being quilted. Do not fold and stitch the plaice at the end as you did for the herring.

7 Make a second plaice in the same way, if desired, from the remaining materials.

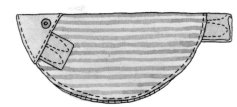

6

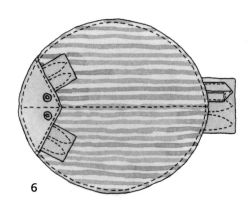

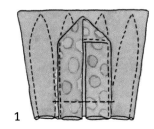

1

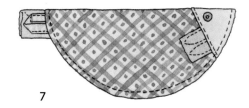

7

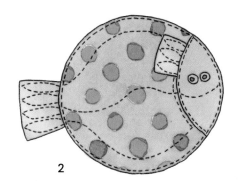

2

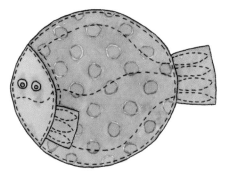

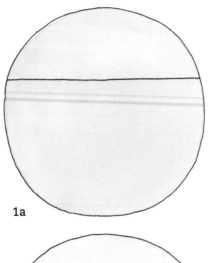

1a

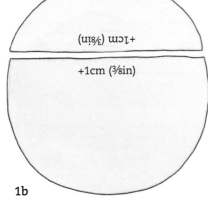

+1cm (⅜in)

+1cm (⅜in)

1b

Herring bags

Here are instructions for two herring bags, one small and one large, both of which have a zip on one side. The small one can be used as a make-up bag or a pencil case and measures 14 x 26cm (5½ x 10in). The large one is 20 x 34cm (8 x 13¼in) and makes an excellent a clutch bag.

For the patterns, see pages 82 and 83.

Materials for one small/large model:

Fabric for the body: 30 x 35cm/ 38 x 45cm (12 x 13¾in/15 x 17¾in)
Lining for the body: 30 x 35cm/ 38 x 45cm (12 x 13¾in/15 x 17¾in)
Fabric for the fins: 10 x 20cm/ 12 x 27cm (4 x 8in/4¾ x 10¾in)
Fabric for the head: 8 x 20cm/ 10 x 22cm (3¼ x 8in/4 x 8¾in)
Fusible wadding: 30 x 35cm/38 x 45cm (12 x 13¾in/15 x 17¾in)
Zip fastener: 30cm/40cm (12/16in)
Bias fabric or binding: 6.5 x 55cm/ 6.5 x 65cm (2½ x 21¾in/2½ x 25½in)

1 Draw the pattern for the body full size as shown in figure 1a. Draw one dividing line, as shown.

2 Cut the pattern along the dividing line (see figure 1b).

3 Cut the two pattern parts from fabric, lining and wadding, adding 1cm (⅜in) seam allowances along the dividing lines.

4 Iron wadding on to the wrong side of the lining pieces.

5 Place the fabric right sides together with the lining, placing the zip in between. The right side of the zip should be facing the fabric.

6 Sew, taking a presser foot's seam allowance, as shown in figure 2a.

7 Fold the fabric and lining wrong sides together. Finger press the lining tightly away from the zip and topstitch on the right side (see figure 2b).

8 Sew the remaining fabric and lining to the other side of the zip in the same way.

9 Cut out the fins and quilt them as explained on page 75, steps 3–4.

2a

2b

10 Cut out the head and press the seam allowance to the wrong side along the straight sides.

11 Open the zip and sew a few tacking stitches across the zip to hold it.

12 Position the head on the body with the fins underneath and topstitch in place just inside the edge (see figure 3).

13 Quilt along the fish's back and tack on the tail (see figure 4).

14 Fold the body right sides together and fold the bias tape wrong sides together. Sew the bias strip in place around the curved edge, taking a presser foot's seam allowance (see figure 5).

15 Fold the bias strip over the seam allowance, fold the ends in neatly and sew the strip in place with slipstitches, making sure your stitches do not show on the right side of the fish.

16 Turn the fish right side out and sew on buttons as eyes.

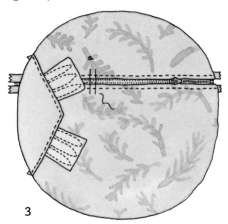

3

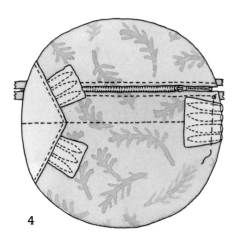

4

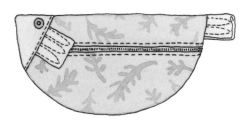

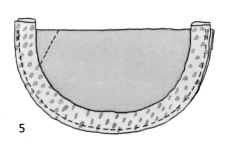

5

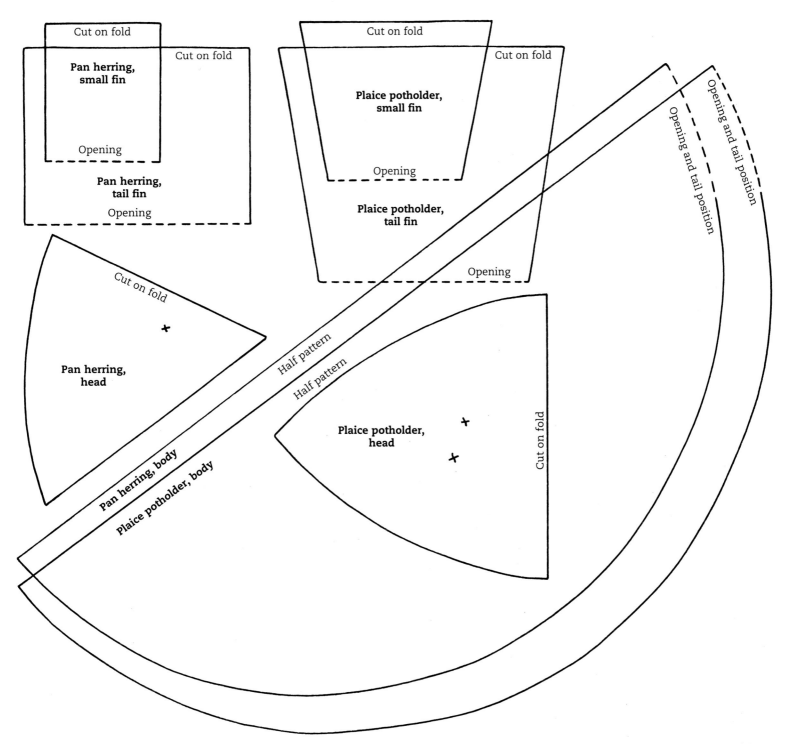

Cut on fold

Pan herring, small fin

Cut on fold

Opening

Pan herring, tail fin

Opening

Cut on fold

Plaice potholder, small fin

Cut on fold

Opening

Plaice potholder, tail fin

Opening

Cut on fold

Pan herring, head

×

Half pattern

Half pattern

Pan herring, body

Plaice potholder, body

Plaice potholder, head

×

×

Cut on fold

Opening and tail position

Opening and tail position

Opening and tail position

81

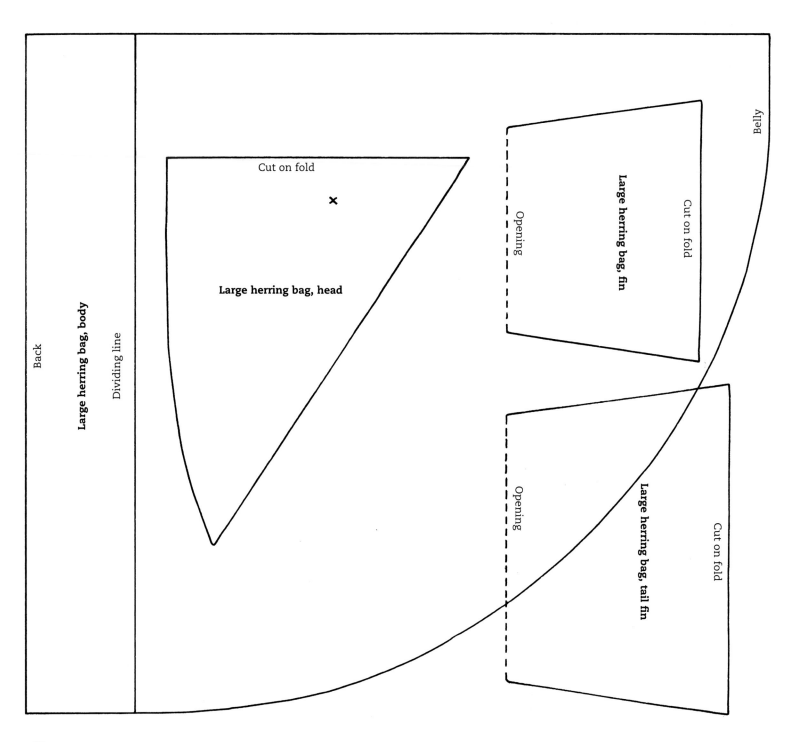

Large herring bag, body

Back

Dividing line

Cut on fold

✗

Large herring bag, head

Opening

Large herring bag, fin

Cut on fold

Belly

Opening

Large herring bag, tail fin

Cut on fold

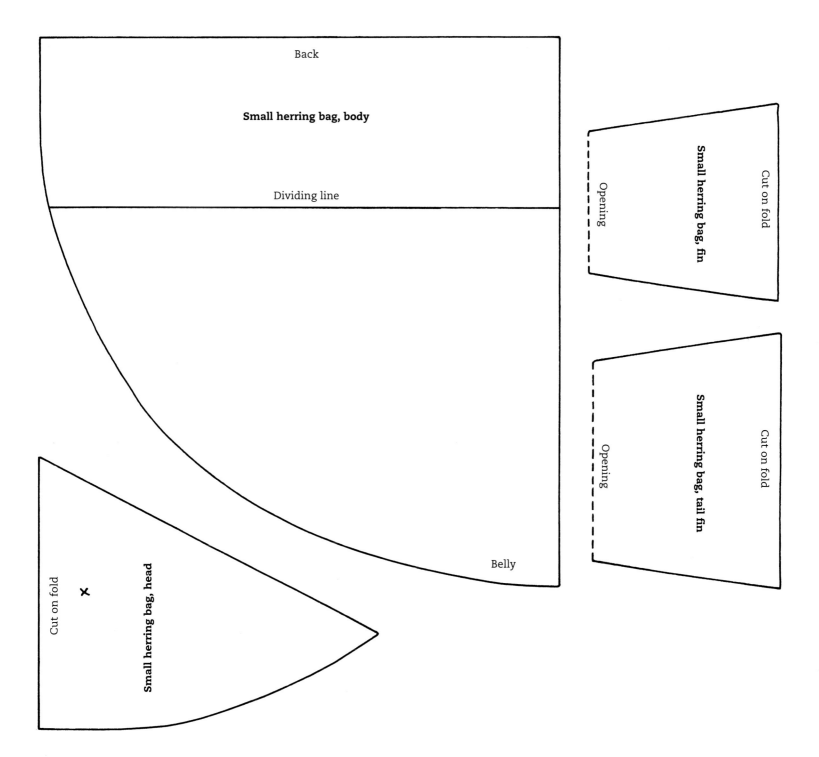

Back

Small herring bag, body

Dividing line

Small herring bag, fin

Opening

Cut on fold

Small herring bag, tail fin

Opening

Cut on fold

Belly

Small herring bag, head

Cut on fold

Happy Hippos

These smart hippos are approximately 45cm (17¾in) tall, and they come to the Ark in their best sailor clothes. For the pattern, see page 90.

Materials for one hippo:
Fabric for the body: 28 x 90cm (11 x 35½in)
Fusible wadding: 10 x 12cm (4 x 4¾in)
Fibrefill
Two buttons for the arms
Two small beads for the eyes (optional)
(Materials for the clothes are given on the following pages.)

1 Draw the patterns full size. Note that the opening for the leg is at the top.
2 Cut a strip of fabric 10 x 28cm (4 x 11in) for the head. Fold it right sides together and sew as shown in figure 1a.
3 Press the seam allowances open and fold the fabric as shown in figure 1b. The seam should be 4.5cm (1¾in) from the bottom fold.
4 Iron the wadding to the back.
5 Draw the head on the fabric so the two dots on the sides of the pattern lie above the seam, and sew the head as shown in figure 1b.
6 Sew one body, two arms, two legs and two ears, as explained on page 9. When cutting out the body, the front body piece should be cut straight as shown in figure 2 (see the pattern).
7 Position the ears in the head and sew them in place with slipstitches.

8 Stuff the head firmly with fibrefill, sew the eyes with French knots or small beads and sew the mouth and nostrils with backstitches.
9 Stuff the arms and legs firmly halfway up and loosely after that.
10 Sew up the openings on the arms with slipstitches.
11 Sew fingers and toes on the arms and legs with backstitches as marked on the pattern.

12 Position the legs right sides together with the front body piece and sew the legs in place, taking a presser foot's seam allowance around the bottom of the body – this provides a marker along which the seam allowances can be folded.
13 Stuff the body very firmly, tuck the seam allowances inside and sew up the opening with slipstitches.

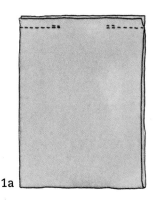

1a

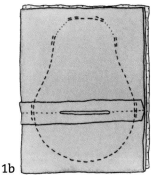

1b

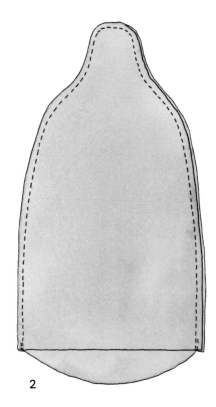

2

14 Put the neck 1.5cm (⅝in) up into the opening on the head and sew the pieces together with slipstitches (see the illustration below).

15 Sew the arms in place on the body with buttons – sew through the body from arm to arm.

Sailor shirt

For the pattern, see page 91.

Materials:
Fabric: 30 x 35cm (12 x 13¾in)
Satin ribbon: 60cm (24in)
Three press-studs
Three small buttons

1 Cut the shirt, two sleeves and a neck facing (only along the outer circle), cutting all parts on the fold as marked on the pattern.

2 Also cut a rectangle for a button placket 7 x 14cm (2¾ x 5½in).

3 Find the shoulder line and centre-front/centre-back lines by folding the fabric right sides together, first one way and then the other (see figure 1).

4 Zigzag around the neck facing and position it right sides together with the shirt.

5 Sew the inner circle of the facing then cut out the neck opening with a 3mm (⅛in) seam allowance; cut small notches as illustrated.

6 Fold the facing towards the wrong side and topstitch it in place.

7 Fold and press a double hem to the right side at the bottom of the shirt and along the edges of the sleeves – first 5mm (¼in) and then 1cm (⅜in).

8 Sew the hems in place with satin ribbon over the top (see figure 2).

9 Mark the centre of the placket and press a 1cm (⅜in) fold to the wrong side along the long edges.

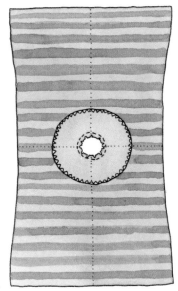

1

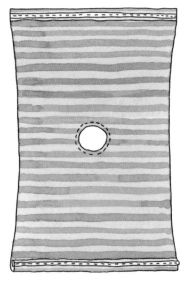

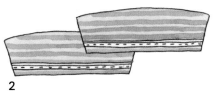

2

10 Position the placket right side against the shirt's wrong side and sew 2mm (¹⁄₁₆in) from the centre mark on each side as shown in figure 3.

11 Cut the placket along the centre marking and trim the ends so that the seam allowance that protrudes over both the neckline and the bottom edge is 7.5mm (a generous ¼in).

12 Fold the sides of the placket to the right side so the finished button plackets will be approximately 1cm (³⁄₈in) wide.

13 Fold the seam allowance at the ends to the wrong side and sew with slipstitches above and below.

14 Sew the button plackets 2mm (¹⁄₁₆in) in from the long edge (see figure 4).

15 Mark and sew three press-studs on the plackets (one part of each press-stud on each placket) and sew three small buttons on the top of the upper placket as decoration (see figure 4).

16 Sew the sleeves to the shirt, right sides together, as shown in figure 5, taking a presser foot's seam allowance and zigzagging the seam allowances together.

17 Fold the shirt right sides together and sew the side and sleeve seams. Cut notches in the seam allowance on the armholes and zigzag the seam allowances together.

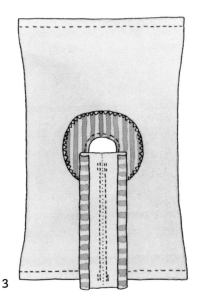

3

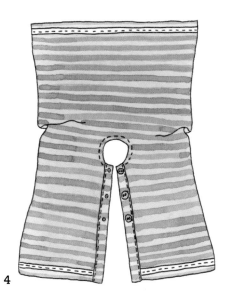

4

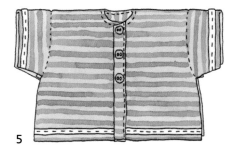

5

Sailor trousers

For the pattern, see page 91.

Materials:

Fabric: 28 x 40cm (11 x 16in)
Satin ribbon: 60cm (24in)
Elastic: 25cm (10in)

1 Cut two trouser legs on the fold as marked on the pattern.
2 Fold 1cm (⅜in) then 2cm (¾in) to the wrong side for bottom hems and sew in place.
3 Sew two strips of satin ribbon on the ends of the legs as shown in figure 1.

4 Place the legs right sides together, sew the centre-front (CF) seam and zigzag the seam allowances together (see figure 1a on page 64).
5 Fold 1cm (⅜in) then 2cm (¾in) to the wrong side at the top (waist) of the trousers and press but do not sew.
6 Open the waist hem and sew the centre-back (CB) seam as in step 4.
7 Refold the waist hem and sew, leaving a small opening so you can thread the elastic through the hem.
8 Place the centre-front and centre-back seams right sides together and then sew the inside-leg seam. Zigzag the seam allowances together.
9 Turn the trousers right side out and thread the elastic through the waist hem (see figure 2).

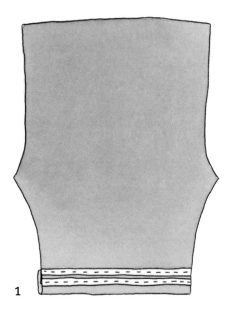

1

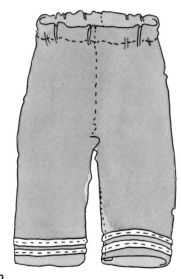

2

Sailor dress

For the pattern, see page 91.

Materials:
Fabric for the bodice: 30 x 35cm (12 x 13¾in)
Fabric for the skirt: 22 x 50cm (8¾ x 19¾in)
Narrow satin ribbon: 180cm (2yd)

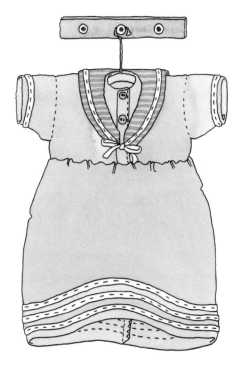

1 Sew the bodice as explained for the shirt on pages 86–87. In this case, the fabric for the plackets is 7 x 10.5cm (2¾ x 4¼in), and the bottom edge should be zigzagged but not hemmed.
2 Fold and press a double hem towards the wrong side along one of the long edges of the skirt fabric (bottom edge). Sew the hem and attach three narrow satin bands.
3 Zigzag the other long edge.
4 Fold the skirt right sides together and sew the centre-back seam, taking a presser foot's seam allowance. Zigzag the seam allowances together.
5 Sew two gathering threads along the top long edge.
6 Pin the skirt right sides together with the bodice, gather the skirt and spread the gathers evenly as shown in figure 2b on page 64.
7 Sew the bodice and the skirt together, taking a presser foot's seam allowance, and then remove the gathering threads.

Sailor collar

For the pattern, see page 91.

Materials:
Fabric: 10.5 x 29cm (4¼ x 11½in)
Satin ribbon: 60cm (24in)

1 Fold the fabric in half with right sides facing, draw the collar pattern on top and stitch along the line as explained on page 9 (see the illustration below).
2 Trim the seam allowance back to 3mm (⅛in), except by the opening where it should be 5mm (¼in).
3 Turn the collar right side out and sew up the opening with slipstitches.
4 Position the satin ribbon 4–5mm (a scant ¼in) from the outer edge of the collar, so there is about 12cm (4¾in) hanging free at each collar point (see the illustration below).
5 Sew the ribbon in place with small running stitches or backstitches – try to avoid the stitches becoming visible on the back of the collar.

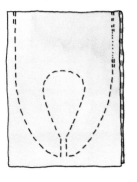

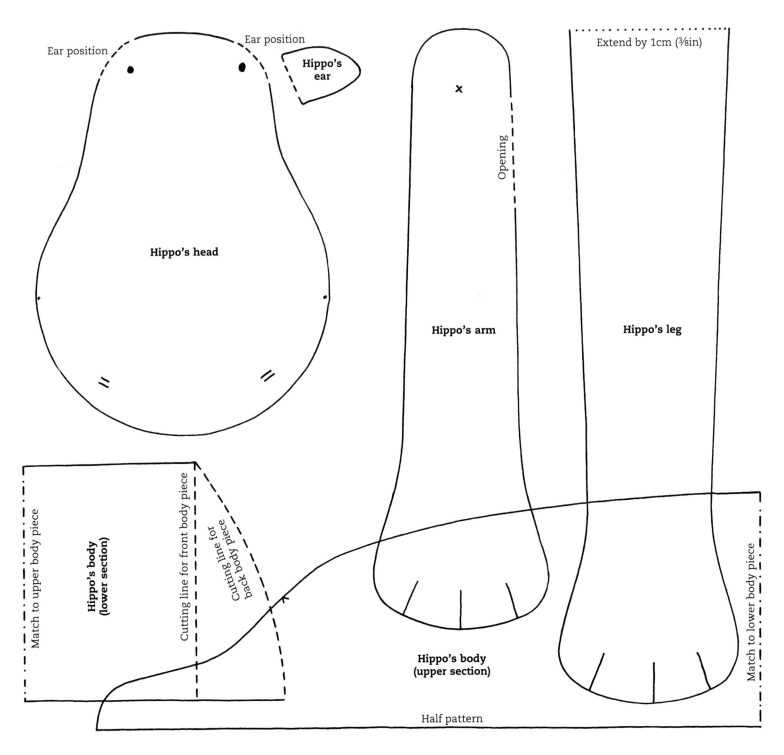

Ear position

Ear position

Hippo's ear

Hippo's head

Opening

Hippo's arm

Extend by 1cm (⅜in)

Hippo's leg

Match to upper body piece

Hippo's body (lower section)

Cutting line for front body piece

Cutting line for back body piece

Match to lower body piece

Hippo's body (upper section)

Half pattern

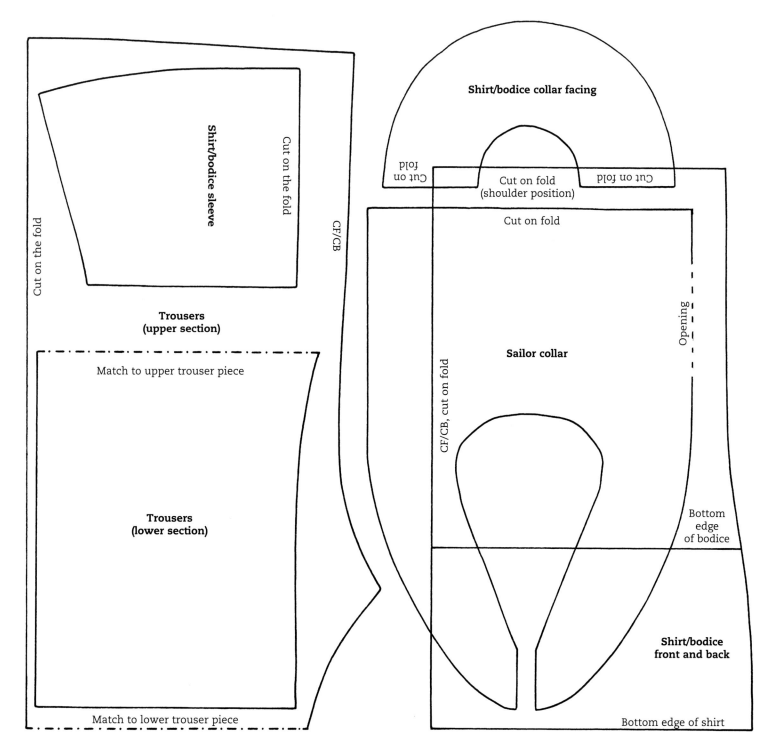

Shirt/bodice collar facing

Cut on the fold

Cut on the fold

Shirt/bodice sleeve

Cut on the fold

CF/CB

**Trousers
(upper section)**

Match to upper trouser piece

**Trousers
(lower section)**

Match to lower trouser piece

Cut on
fold

Cut on fold
(shoulder position)

Cut on
fold

Cut on fold

Opening

Sailor collar

CF/CB, cut on fold

Bottom
edge
of bodice

**Shirt/bodice
front and back**

Bottom edge of shirt

Graceful Giraffes

The giraffes are far-sighted in more ways than one, having put on their swimsuits and brought a beach ball and a bath duck with them on to the Ark. Their arms and legs are sewn using the same pattern, but when the pattern of the leg is drawn, 20cm (8in) should be added between the two continuation lines, so the leg will be a total of 50cm (19¾in) long. The giraffes are approximately 87cm (34¼in) tall. For the pattern, see page 97.

Materials for one giraffe:
Fabric for the body: 50 x 60cm (19¾ x 24in)
Fabric for the hands and feet: 6.5 x 38cm (2½ x 15in)
Fabric for the horns: 5 x 7cm (2 x 2¾in)
Four buttons for the arms and legs
Fibrefill
(Materials for the bathing suits are given on page 94.)

1 Draw the patterns full size.
2 Cut a piece of body fabric 50 x 38cm (19¾ x 15in) for the arms and legs.
3 Sew the piece to the fabric for the hands and feet with right sides facing, press the seam allowances towards the hands/feet, and topstitch in place.
4 Fold the remaining body fabric and the newly joined fabric right sides together, draw a body, two ears, two arms and two legs on the respective fabrics and sew as explained on page 9.
5 Stuff the body very firmly and sew up the opening with slipstitches.
6 Stuff the arms and legs very firmly up to 12cm (4¾in) and 21cm (8¼in) respectively and tie a knot in both arms and legs.

7 Loosely stuff each limb above the knot and sew up the openings on the arms, legs and ears with slipstitches.
8 Divide the fabric for the horns into two pieces 5 x 3.5cm (2 x 1⅜in), fold the pieces and sew them together with slipstitches as shown in figures 1a–1c.
9 Sew the ears on the head so they meet behind the head (see figure 2b).
10 Sew on the horns with slipstitches between the ears (see figures 2a and 2b).
11 Sew the eyes and nostrils with French knots and the mouth with backstitches.
12 Sew the arms and legs in place on the body with buttons – sew through the body from arm to arm and from leg to leg.

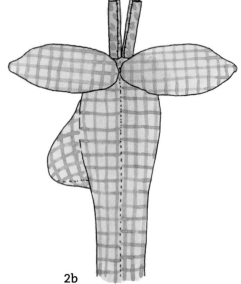

2b

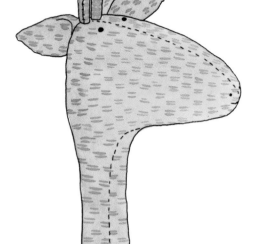

2a

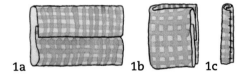

1a   1b   1c

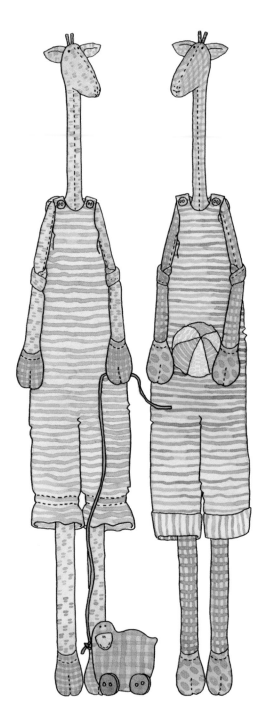

Bathing suits

The bathing suits can be sewn with an added turn-up at the bottom of each leg or with an elasticised channel. For the pattern, see page 98.

Materials for one costume:
Fabric for costume: 50 x 60cm (20 x 24in)
Fabric for the turn-ups (boy): 7.5 x 24cm (3 x 9½in)
Elastic (girl): 12cm (4¾in)
Two buttons for shoulder straps

1 Draw the patterns full size.
2 Cut a front piece and a back piece with the centre-front/centre-back lines on the fold. Cut two facings, also on the fold.
3 Zigzag the straight bottom edge of each facing. Place one facing, right sides together with the front piece, and one facing right sides together with the back piece. Sew as shown in figure 1, taking a presser foot's seam allowance.
4 Trim the seam allowances back to 3mm (⅛in) and cut small notches in the curves for ease.
5 Fold the facing up as shown in figure 2, place the front and back pieces right sides together and sew the side seams. Zigzag the raw edges of the seam allowances together.

1

6 Turn the costume right side out and topstitch along the armholes and neckline as shown in figure 3.

7 For turn-ups, cut the fabric for the turn-ups into two pieces, each 7.5 x 12cm (3 x 4¾in). Fold each piece wrong sides together and position one right sides together with each of the leg ends (see figure 3). Sew the turn-ups in place, taking a presser foot's seam allowance. Zigzag the raw edges of the seam allowances together. Alternatively, for elasticised legs, zigzag the raw edges at the bottom of the trousers to neaten them. Fold 3cm (1¼in) to the wrong side and sew the hems with two lines of stitching, forming a drawstring casing (see figure 4). Divide the elastic into two and thread a length through each drawstring casing.

8 Place the centre-front (CF) and centre-back (CB) seams right sides together and sew the inside-leg seam – if you are using elastic in the legs, pull it taut before catching the ends in the seam. Zigzag the raw edges of the seam allowances together.

9 Put the bathing costume on the giraffe and join the shoulder edges together with a button.

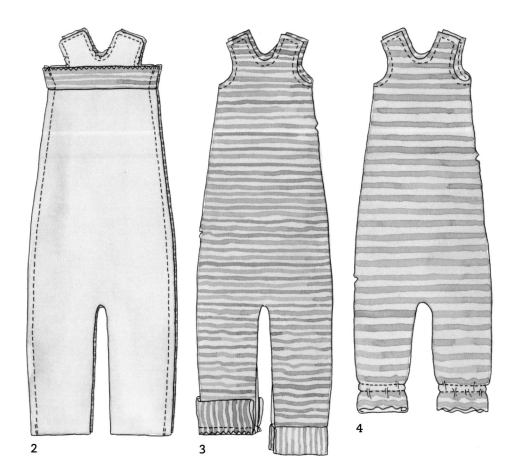

2

3

4

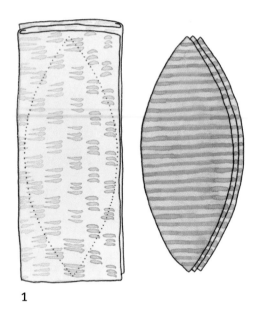

1

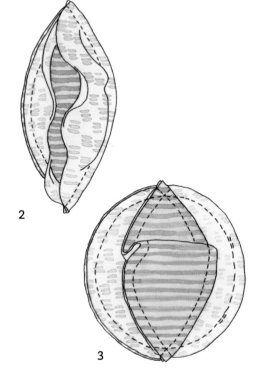

2

3

Beach ball

This beach ball can be sewn from two or more different fabrics. Two fabrics give a traditional look.
For the pattern, see page 98.

Materials:
Two different fabrics: each 14 x 20cm (5½ x 8in)
Fibrefill

1 Fold the fabric pieces into three as shown in figure 1 and cut the ball segment through all the layers.
2 Sew two half balls consisting of three alternating fabric segments as shown in figure 2.
3 Tack to mark the opening.
4 Sew the two halves right sides together as shown in figure 3. Turn the ball right side out and stuff it very firmly with fibrefill. Sew up the opening with slipstitches.

Companion duck

For the pattern, see page 98.

Materials:
Fabric for the duck: 10 x 20cm (4 x 8in)
Fabric for the beak: 4 x 7cm (1½ x 2¾in)
Four buttons for wheels

1 Sew the body and beak as explained on page 9.
2 Cut a small slit at the back of the beak for turning and stuffing.
3 Stuff each piece firmly with fibrefill and sew up the opening with slipstitches.
4 Sew the eyes with French knots and add nasal slits and a smile on the beak with backstitches.
5 Appliqué the beak on to the body.
6 Sew buttons on each side of the body as wheels (see the illustration below).

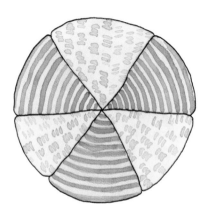

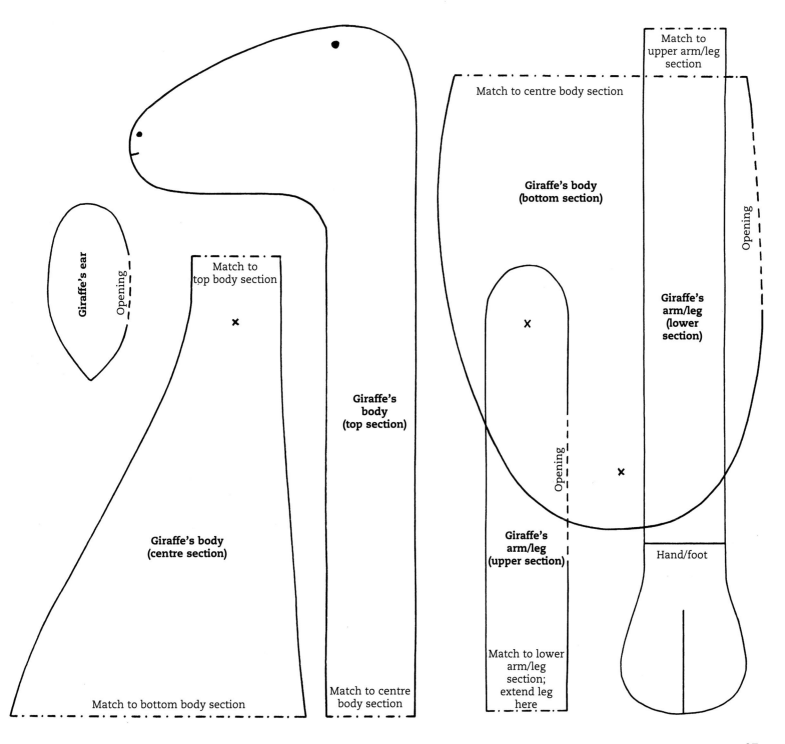

Giraffe's ear

Opening

Match to
top body section

✗

Giraffe's body
(centre section)

Giraffe's
body
(top section)

Match to bottom body section

Match to centre
body section

Match to centre body section

Match to
upper arm/leg
section

Giraffe's body
(bottom section)

Opening

✗

Giraffe's
arm/leg
(lower
section)

Opening

✗

Giraffe's
arm/leg
(upper section)

Match to lower
arm/leg
section;
extend leg
here

Hand/foot

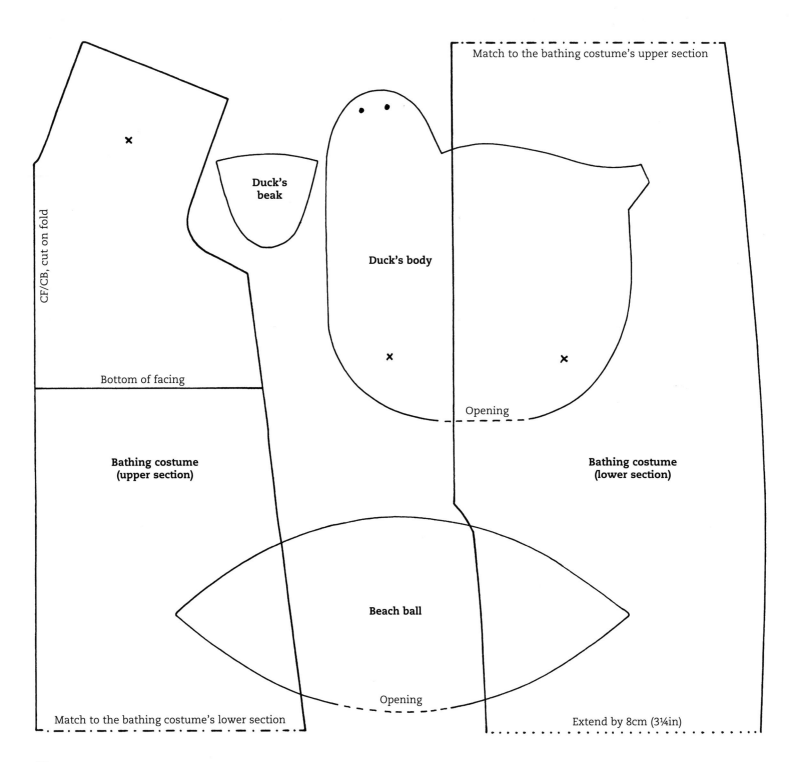

Match to the bathing costume's upper section

CF/CB, cut on fold

Duck's beak

Duck's body

Bottom of facing

Bathing costume
(upper section)

Opening

Bathing costume
(lower section)

Beach ball

Opening

Match to the bathing costume's lower section

Extend by 8cm (3¼in)

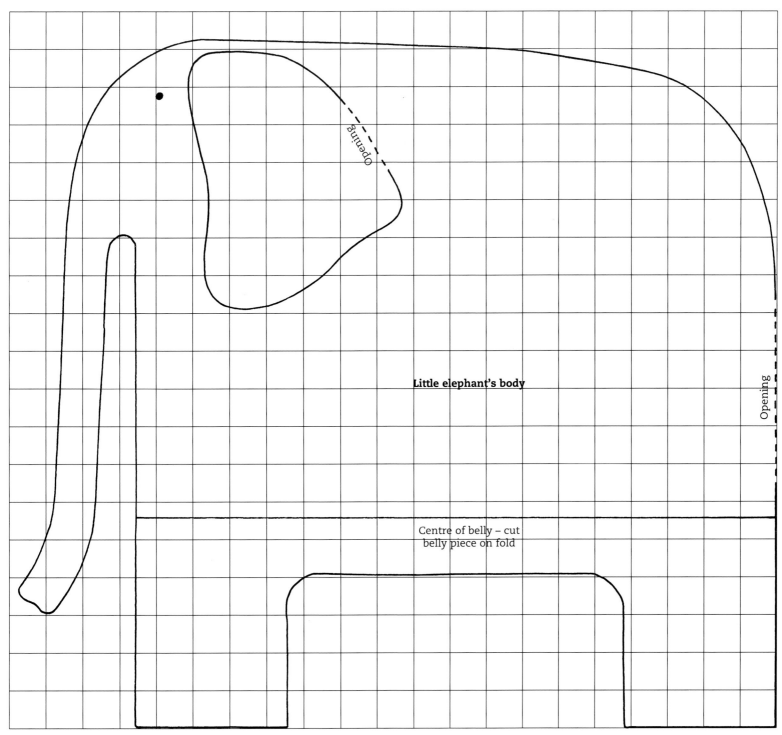

Opening

Opening

Little elephant's body

Centre of belly – cut
belly piece on fold

To enlarge the pattern for a big elephant, 1 square = 2.5cm (1in)

Elephant Family

The elephants are sewn in two sizes: the little (baby) one is 18cm (7in) tall while the big one (parent) is 45cm (17¾in) tall. Instructions for the big elephant begin on page 102. For the pattern, see page 99.

Little elephant

Materials for one elephant:
Fabric: 35 x 60cm (13¾ x 23¾in)
Fibrefill
Two small buttons for eyes

1 Cut fabric pieces 23 x 40cm (9 x 16in) for the body, 14 x 23cm (5½ x 9in) for the belly and 3.5 x 12cm (1¼ x 4¾in) for the tail. The remaining fabric should be folded right sides together so you can cut out two pairs of ears.

2 Fold the fabric for the body and the belly separately, right sides together, as shown in figure 1. Draw the pattern on each piece and add a seam allowance around the legs as illustrated.

3 Sew the body from the belly-fold marking on one side to the belly-fold marking on the other side, as shown in figure 1.

4 Cut out the body, adding a 3–4mm (⅛in) seam allowance, except at the opening where it should be 1cm (⅜in).

5 Cut out the legs and belly with the added seam allowance.

6 Fold up the legs of the body piece and place the belly right sides together with it as shown in figure 2.

7 Sew as shown from belly fold to belly fold.

8 Turn the elephant round and sew the other two legs (see figure 3).

9 Trim the seam allowance around the legs back to 3–4mm (⅛in) and zigzag the seam allowances together.

10 Turn the elephant right side out and stuff it with fibrefill.

11 Sew up the opening with slipstitches.

12 Make two ears as explained on page 9.

13 Appliqué the ears on to the elephant and sew on buttons for the eyes.

14 Fray approximately 1.5cm (⅝in) of the tail fabric at one end, fold and sew the tail as shown in figure 4. The seam allowance should be trimmed back to 3–4mm (⅛in) to make it easier to turn out.

15 Turn the tail right side out and sew it on.

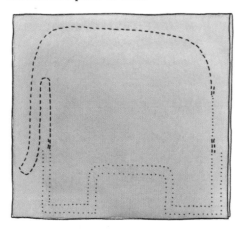

1

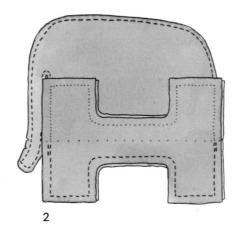

2

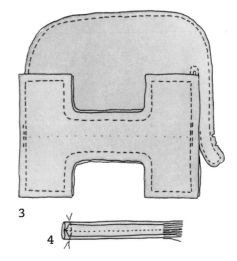

3

4

Big elephant

The big elephant is sewn in basically the same way as the little elephant but the pattern on page 99 should be enlarged by 250%. This means that each square is equivalent to 2.5cm (1in).

For the big elephant, a zip is sewn on in the belly piece and the body is filled with a homemade cushion pad. So that the elephant can stand, small pellet bags are sewn and put in the legs.

Materials for one elephant:

Fabric for the elephant: 75 x 130cm (29½ x 51in)
Fabric for a cushion pad: 38 x 95cm (15 x 37½in)
Fabric for foot pads: 24 x 62cm (9½ x 24½in)
Zip fastener: 50cm (20in)
Two small buttons for eyes
Fibrefill
Pellets

1 Cut fabric pieces 55 x 97cm (21¾ x 38¼in) for the body, 33 x 55cm (13 x 21¾in) for the belly and 7 x 30cm (2¾ x 12in) for the tail. The remaining fabric should be folded right sides together so you can cut out two pairs of ears.

2 Fold the fabric pieces for the body and belly as shown in figure 1 on page 100.

3 Cut the belly pattern on the fold and add 1cm (⅜in) seam allowances along all sides of the belly and legs.

4 Zigzag the edge of the belly pieces along the dividing lines.

5 Attach the belly pieces to the zip as explained on page 10.

6 Sew the elephant as explained on page 100, but without leaving an opening. All the seam allowances must be cut back to 1cm (⅜in); slightly narrower around the trunk.

7 Stuff fibrefill in the trunk.

8 Fold the cushion-pad fabric right sides together so it measures 38 x 47.5cm (15 x 18¾in) and make a cushion pad, as explained on page 10.

9 Stuff the elephant with the cushion pad.

10 Cut the foot-pad fabric into two pieces, each 12 x 62cm (4¾ x 24½in). Fold each piece right sides together and sew as shown in figures 1a and 1b (right). The opening should be about 5cm (2in) long.

11 Turn the fabric right side out, put pellets in each end and sew up the opening with slipstitches.

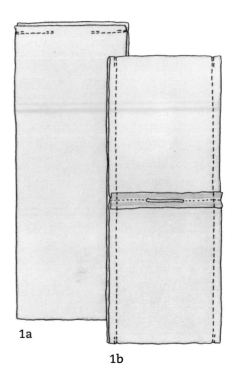

1a

1b

2

12 Topstitch 2cm (¾in) from the centre of each bag on each side to enclose the pellets as shown in figure 2.

13 Slip the bags into the elephant's forelegs and hind legs.

Patchwork Picnic Blanket

This pretty patchwork is approximately 135cm (53in) square, but it can easily be enlarged, if required, either by cutting larger squares or by using more squares. The blanket is backed with fleece so that it is extra soft. Do not reserve it just for picnics – it is wonderful as a cosy blanket to snuggle under in front of the television.

Materials:

Fabric for 16 squares: each 35 x 35cm
  (13¾ x 13¾in)
Fleece for backing: 150 x 150cm
  (59 x 59in)
Fabric for binding: 7.5cm x 5.5m
  (3in x 6yd) – join pieces as necessary

1 Cut 16 squares 35 x 35cm (13¾ x 13¾in) from different fabrics.
2 Arrange the squares in four rows with four squares in each row.
3 Sew the squares together in rows with right sides facing. Press the seam allowances to one side so that all the seam allowances in one row go one way, and all the seam allowances in the next row go the other way (see figure 1). This reduces bulk at the seam allowances.

4 Sew the rows together with right sides facing.
5 Position the patchwork wrong sides together with the fleece and tack the layers together.
6 Square up the edges by trimming, if necessary. Quilt as shown in figure 2.
7 Sew the binding on the blanket's right side, then fold it over to the back and slipstitch it in place as explained on page 30.
8 Remove the tacking threads to finish.

1

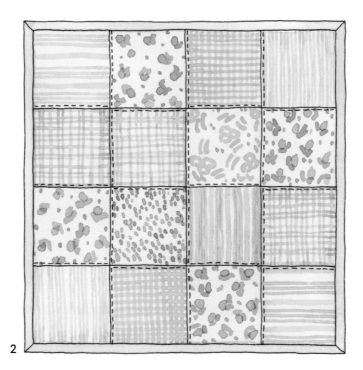

2

Seat Cushion

This seat cushion measures 40 x 40cm (15¾ x 15¾in) and has a carrying handle to make it easy to transport for a picnic. What is more, it can be fitted with one or two pockets, so you can carry miscellaneous small items too. A piece of mattress pad (folded to the correct size), a foam cushion or a homemade cushion pad can be used as filling.

The cushion layers are 'quilted' in four places and the cushion is decorated with homemade fabric buttons.

Materials for one cushion:
Fabric for the cushion: 45.5 x 89.5cm (18 x 35¼in)
Fabric for the handle: 12 x 23cm (4¾ x 9in)
Fabric for a large pocket: 27 x 32cm (10¾ x 12¾in)
Fabric for a small pocket: 20 x 25cm (8 x 10in)
Fabric for buttons: 10 x 25cm (4 x 10in)
Mattress pad: 84 x 84cm (33 x 33in); alternatively use a 40 x 40cm (15¾ x 15¾in) foam cushion or make a cushion pad (see page 10)
Fibrefill for the buttons

1 Fold and sew a handle as shown in figures 1a and 1b.
2 Position the handle in the centre of the cushion fabric and sew it in place (see figure 2).
3 Fold a 3cm (1¼in) double hem along the top edge of each pocket, sew the hem in place and then topstitch the hem.
4 Zigzag the three raw edges of each pocket and press about 1cm (⅜in) to the wrong side along these edges.
5 Sew the small pocket to the large pocket, topstitching around the folded edges as shown in figure 3.

6 Position the large pocket on the cushion fabric 6.5cm (2½in) below the handle and topstitch it in place around the folded edges.
7 Fold the cushion fabric right sides together and sew the three sides, leaving a 20cm (8in) opening to turn through as shown in figure 4.
8 Press (as well as possible) the seam allowances open and sew the corners as shown in figure 5. The length of the stitching should be 3–4cm (1¼–1½in), depending on the filling.
9 Trim the excess fabric at each corner and zigzag over the raw edges.

1a

1b

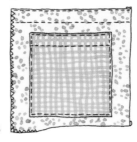
3

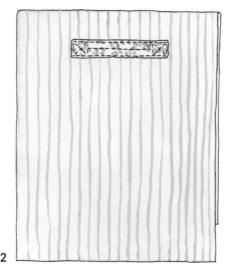
2

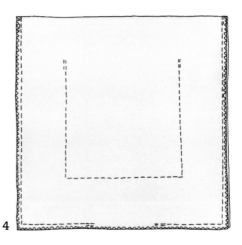
4

10 Turn the cushion right side out through the gap.

11 Fold the mattress pad as shown in figure 6 and sew overcast stitches over the folds. Alternatively, use a 40 x 40cm (15¾ x 15¾in) foam cushion, or make a 40 x 40cm (15¾ x 15¾in) cushion pad as explained on page 10.

12 Fill the cushion and sew up the opening with slipstitches.

13 Fold the fabric for the buttons as shown in figure 7a and press it. Draw 4 or 5 buttons on top, using the template given here.

14 Sew along each drawn circle then cut out the circles, adding a 3mm (⅛in) seam allowance (see figure 7b). Turn each circle right side out.

15 Stuff the round buttons with fibrefill and sew up the opening with slipstitches (see figure 7c).

16 Hand stitch around the edge of each button in six places with the button's centre at the point where the stitch emerges (see figures 7d and 7e). Tighten each stitch as you go, so the button becomes flower-shaped.

17 Position four buttons as shown in the illustration below, avoiding the pockets, and stitch in place through all the layers to finish.

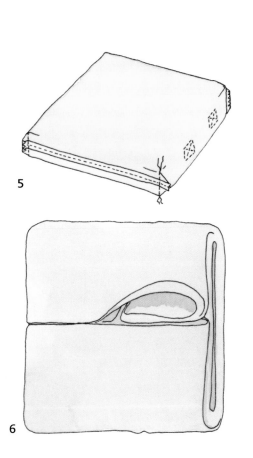

5

6

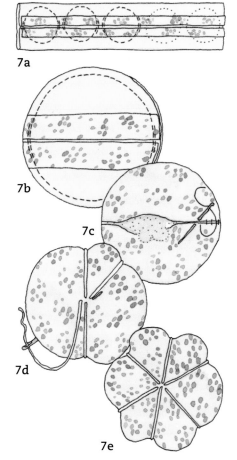

7a

7b

7c

7d

7e

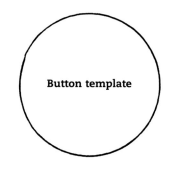

Button template

Sunhat

This pretty hat is a statement that summer has really arrived. It has an inside circumference of 59cm (23¼in) and can be made with either a wide or narrow brim. To make a hat that is larger or smaller, divide the crown and brim along the half-pattern line and adjust the pattern along this edge (see figures 1a and 1b).
For the pattern, see page 108.

Materials:
Fabric: 60 x 80cm (23½ x 31½in)

1 Draw the pattern full size.
2 Fold the fabric right sides together, so the short side is halved.
3 Cut two brims on the fold as marked on the pattern and cut out five crown pieces from the remaining fabric.
4 Sew the brim pieces together separately along the centre-back seam and press the seam allowances open (see figure 2).

5 Place the brims right sides together and sew the outer edge as shown in figure 3.
6 Trim the seam allowance back to 3mm (⅛in) and turn right side out.
7 Sew lines of topstitching 1cm (⅜in) apart over the brim (see figure 4).
8 Zigzag the curved raw edges of the crown pieces.
9 Sew four crown pieces together in pairs, right sides together (see figure 5).
10 Press the seam allowances open and topstitch them in place, or zigzag the seam allowances together then press them to one side and topstitch them in place.
11 Sew the last crown piece right sides together with one of the pairs and topstitch the seam allowances in place as just explained (see figure 6). Sew the two sections right sides together and topstitch or zigzag the seam allowances as before.
12 Divide both the crown and the brim into four equal parts.

2

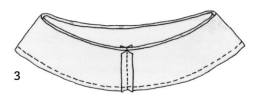

3

4

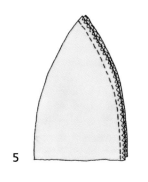

5

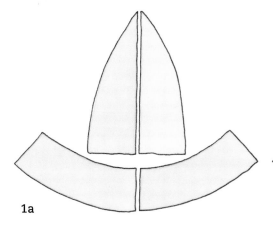

1a

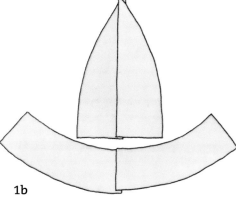

1b

6

13 Pin the crown to the brim with right sides facing, matching your marks, and sew them together (see figure 7).
14 Zigzag the raw edges together, press the seam allowances up into the crown and topstitch in place from the right side.

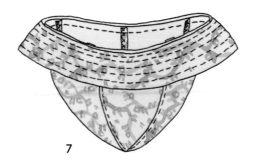

7

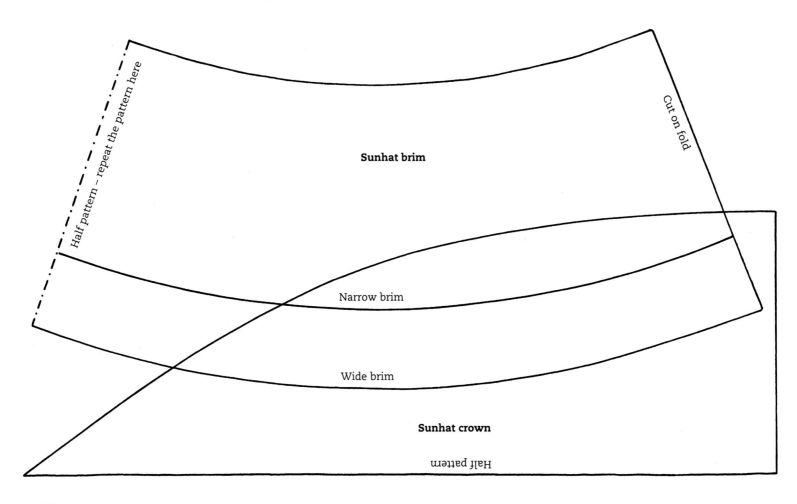

Half pattern – repeat the pattern here

Cut on fold

Sunhat brim

Narrow brim

Wide brim

Sunhat crown

Half pattern

Basket Lining

This scallop-edged lining is suitable for either a round or square basket.
For a simple, straight-sided basket without a handle see the instructions below. If the basket has a handle, see page 111, and if it also has sloping sides, see page 112.

Materials:
A round or square basket
Fabric for the main section (see steps 1–3) and for the edging

1 Measure the distance around the basket's top edge (see figure 1). Add 1.5cm (⅝in) for seam allowances.
2 Measure the basket's external height plus half the bottom width (see

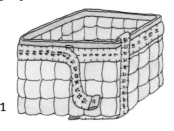

figure 1). Add 1.5cm (⅝in) for seam allowances to this too.
3 Cut a piece of fabric to the resulting measurements.
4 Fold the fabric right sides together, so the longest side is halved.
5 Sew the side seam, taking a presser foot's seam allowance. Zigzag the raw edges together (see figure 2), press the seam allowances to one side and topstitch them in place.
6 Cut a 12.5cm (5in) edging strip using the scalloped pattern on page 112 – the length of the strip should correspond to the basket's circumference plus seam allowance (see step 1). Alternatively, you can use a straight strip, as shown in the picture on page 115.
7 Press the edging fabric wrong sides together lengthwise. Unfold the strip and press a seam allowance towards the wrong side along one long edge. Unfold the strip and sew the ends right sides together to form a ring, taking a presser foot's seam allowance.
8 Press the seam allowances open (see figure 3).

9 Fold the fabric right sides together and draw the scallops on top, placing them with the curves facing the folded fabric edge. Sew along the curves (see figure 4).
10 Cut out the scallops with a 3mm (⅛in) seam allowance and turn right side out.
11 One edge of the strip has been pre-folded; sew the other edge with its right side against the main fabric's wrong side, taking a presser foot's seam allowance. Press the seam allowance towards the edging fabric.
12 Fold the edging over to the right side of the main piece. Refold the narrow hem so it just covers the stitching and topstitch the edge in place.
13 Turn the basket lining wrong side out and divide the fabric into four equal parts, marking with pins (see figure 5).
14 Fold pleats as shown in figure 6.
15 Sew the pleats, taking a presser foot's seam allowance, and zigzag the raw edges together (see figure 7).
16 Put the cover in the basket with the wrong side towards the basket and turn the wavy edging out over the rim.

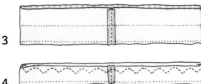

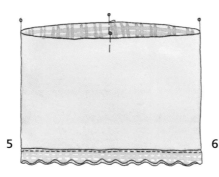

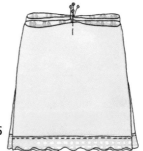

Lining for a basket with a handle

A traditional splint basket with a handle, like the one pictured below, usually has a rectangular shape with straight sides. The following instructions explain how to make a lining for this type of basket.
The pattern for the scalloped edging is given on page 114.

Materials:

A basket with a handle
Fabric for the main section (see steps 1–3), for the edging and bias strip

1 Measure the external circumference of the basket around the top edge (see figure 1 on the previous page). Add 1.5cm (⅝in) for seam allowances

to this measurement. Press the measuring tape down as far as possible between the edge and the handle when measuring.
2 Measure the basket's external height plus half the bottom width. Take the measurement outside the handle. Add 1.5cm (⅝in) for seam allowances to this too.
3 Cut a piece of fabric to the resulting measurements.
4 Fold the fabric right sides together, so the longest side is halved.
5 Sew the side seam, taking a presser foot's seam allowance. Zigzag the raw edges together (see figure 2 on the previous page), press the seam allowances to one side and topstitch them in place.
6 Calculate the length of the edging by measuring from handle to handle and adding 1.5cm (⅝in) for seam allowances. The strip for the edging should be 12.5cm (5in) wide. Cut two strips with the calculated length.
7 Sew the edgings as explained on the previous page and turn right side out.
8 Mark the position of the handle on the lining with pins and position the

two edging pieces right sides together with the lining (see figure 1).
9 Cut a 4cm (1½in) bias strip to the same length as the circumference of the basket lining (including seam allowances), press a seam allowance to the wrong side along one long edge and sew the strip ends together with right sides facing, taking a presser foot's seam allowance.
10 Position the binding right sides together with the basket lining, with the edging pieces in between, and sew in place, taking a presser foot's seam allowance (see figure 2).
11 Turn wrong side out, fold the bias strip down over the basket lining and topstitch the strip in place as shown in figure 3.
12 Using pins, divide the lining into four parts corresponding to the measurement of the bottom of the basket (see figure 4).
13 Fold pleats as shown in figure 4 and then stitch, taking a presser foot's seam allowance. Zigzag the raw edges together as shown in figure 7 on the previous page.

1

2

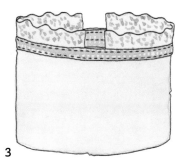

3

4

Basket with handle and sloping sides

If the basket has sloping sides, a paper pattern must be made for the sides and bottom sections. Here are a few tips on how to do this – and then you will have to draw on a little patience! It could be a good idea to sew a sample lining from an old piece of fabric. The pattern for the scalloped edging is given on page 114.

Materials:

A basket with a handle and sloping sides
Fabric for the main section (see steps 1–6), for the edging and bias strip

1 Divide the edge of the basket into four equal parts and mark with tape or chalk.

2 Dampen a page of newspaper lightly with a water spray and carefully shape the paper to fit the basket between two of the side markers (i.e. from handle to handle).

3 Draw the shape on the pattern paper. Since the fabric has to go beyond the edge of the basket, measure the external circumference, and add this additional width. Also add 1.5cm (⅝in) for seam allowances to the height and width.

4 Cut the pattern from a double layer of fabric (see figure 1).

5 Draw a pattern for the bottom to the dimensions of the external bottom of the basket. Test the pattern inside the basket and add seam allowances if necessary.

6 Cut a bottom piece in a single layer of fabric.

7 Sew the side seams of the lining, taking a presser foot's seam allowance. Zigzag the raw edges, press the seam allowances to one side and topstitch them in place.

8 Sew the bottom piece right sides together with the side piece, taking a presser foot's seam allowance. Zigzag the raw edges together, press the seam allowances to one side and topstitch them in place (see figure 2).

9 Calculate the size of the edging and attach it with a bias strip as explained on the previous page.

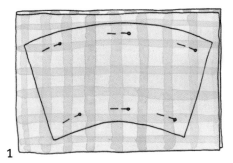

1

2

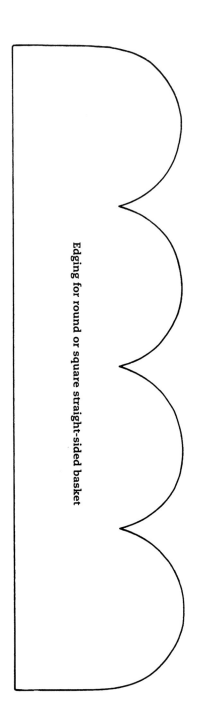

Edging for round or square straight-sided basket

Cutlery Roll

This useful addition to the picnic basket is intended for four sets of cutlery, but the model can easily be expanded. It measures 26 x 30cm (10¼ x 12in).

The pattern for the scalloped edging is given on page 114.

Materials:

Fabric for the scalloped edging: two pieces, each 8.5 x 32cm (3¼ x 12½in)

Fabric for a ribbon tie: 8 x 85cm (3 x 33½in)

Fabric for the outside: 32 x 45cm (12½ x 17¾in)

Fabric for the inside: two pieces, each 32 x 23.5cm (12½ x 9¼in)

Fusible wadding for the edging: two pieces, each 4 x 32cm (1½ x 12½in)

Fusible wadding for the outside: 32 x 45cm (12½ x 17¾in)

1 Fold the strips for the scalloped edging right sides together and draw eight scallops using the pattern on page 114.

2 Iron fusible wadding to the back of each strip and sew along the drawn line as shown in figure 1.

3 Cut out the scallops with a 3mm (⅛in) seam allowance and turn right side out.

4 Fold and then sew the ribbon tie as shown in figure 2.

5 Iron the remaining wadding to the outside fabric's wrong side.

6 Place the two pieces of fabric for the inside of the cutlery roll right sides together and sew together, taking a presser foot's seam allowance and leaving an opening in the centre about 12cm (4¾in) long, as shown in figure 3.

7 Press the seam allowances open.

8 Place the outside and inside fabrics right sides together with the wavy edges in between and sew both ends, taking a presser foot's seam allowance (see figure 4).

9 Turn right side out and topstitch along the bottom edge (see figure 5).

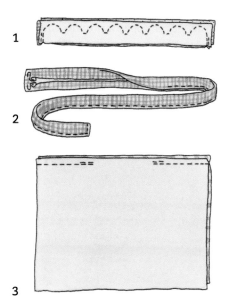

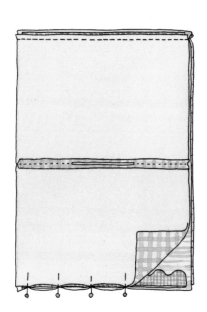

10 Place the ribbon tie 10.5cm (4¼in) from the upper wavy edge and sew as shown. The tape may only be sewn in place on the outside fabric.

11 Fold a 19.5cm (7¾in) deep pocket and hold the top three layers together with pins (see figure 6).

12 Turn wrong side out and sew the side seams, taking a presser foot's seam allowance (see figure 7).

13 Turn right side out and sew up the opening with slipstitches.

14 Topstitch under the top scalloped edge.

15 Mark and sew three lines of stitches to make four pockets, while holding the ribbon tie in place with pins (see figure 8). Remove the pins.

5

6

7

8

Scalloped edging

Edge for cutlery roll

Edge for basket lining (baskets with handles)

Insulated Bottle Bag

This useful bottle bag is lined with insulated wadding to keep a chilled bottle of squash or wine cool for a couple of hours. It measures 15 x 41cm (6 x 16¼in).

Materials:
Fabric for the outer bag: 18 x 75cm (7 x 29½in)
Fabric for the lining: 18 x 75cm (7 x 29½in)
Fabric for the scalloped edging: two pieces, each 13 x 18cm (5 x 7in)
Fabric for the ribbon tie: 8 x 75cm (3 x 29½in)
Insulated wadding: 18 x 75cm (7 x 29½in)

1 Fold the strips for the scalloped edging right sides together, draw four scallops and sew as shown in figure 1a – note that you must not sew right down at the sides.
2 Cut out the scallops with a 3mm (⅛in) seam allowance (see figure 1b).
3 Press the seam allowances to the wrong side on the unstitched side edges of the edging (see figure 1c).
4 Turn right side out and topstitch the folds in place separately and through both layers of fabric 3.5cm (1⅜in) from the raw edges as shown in figure 1d (just below the scallops). This will form one side of the channel for the ribbon drawstring.

5 Fold and sew the ribbon as shown in figure 2 on page 113.
6 Place the outer fabric's wrong side against the insulated wadding and fold it right sides together, so the longest side is halved.
7 Sew side seams as shown in figure 2.
8 Fold the lining fabric right sides together in the same way and sew the side seams with an opening in one side about 12cm (4¾in) long (see figure 3).
9 Trim the seam allowance back to 3mm (⅛in), except by the opening where it should be 5mm (¼in).
10 Turn the outer bag right side out.

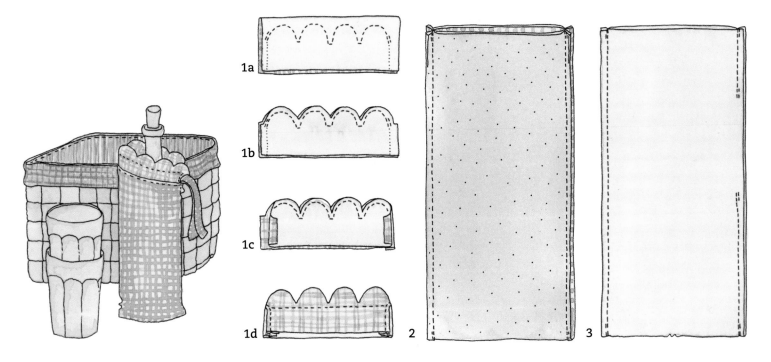

1a
1b
1c
1d
2
3

11 Position the scalloped edging right sides together with the edge of the outer bag (see figure 4).

12 Pull the bag lining right sides together with the outer bag and sew together along the top, taking a presser foot's seam allowance (see figure 5).

13 Turn right side out and sew up the opening with slipstitches.

14 Stuff the bag lining into the outer bag and thread the ribbon through the channel (see figure 6).

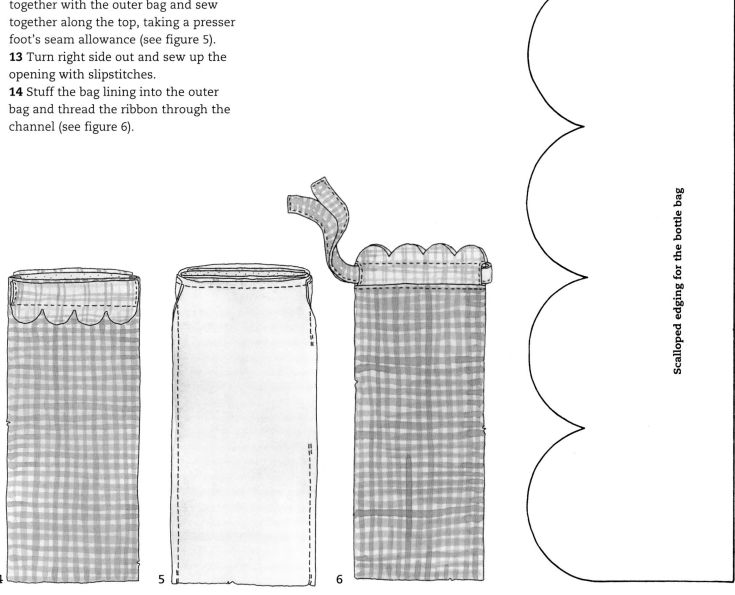

4

5

6

Scalloped edging for the bottle bag

Paper Boats

Haven't most of us, at some point, perhaps long ago, sailed a paper boat down a river, on a pond or even in a bath? All you need is a piece of paper and perhaps a bowl of water to float the boat in.

Materials for one boat:

One sheet of A4 or A5 paper

1 Fold the paper so the longest side is halved, and halve it again along the longest side (see figure 1).

2 Open the last fold and fold the right corner to the centre at the front and the left corner to the centre at the back (see figure 2).

3 Fold the four small corners in as shown in figures 3 and 4.

4 Open and refold the model so the centre fold becomes the side fold (see figure 5).

5 Fold the bottom corners up as shown in figure 6. Open and refold the paper model as you did in step 4 (see figure 7).

6 Open and shape the boat as shown in figures 8 and 9.

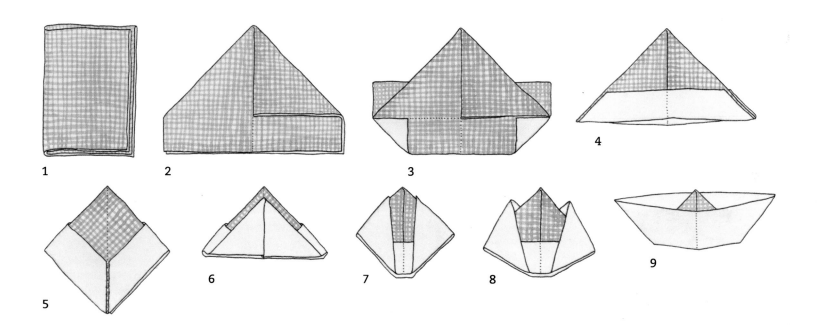

1 2 3 4

5 6 7 8 9

Sweet Treat – Olive Buns

If you are going on a picnic, it is nice to fill the basket with a batch of home-baked buns.

Ingredients for about 25:
25g (1oz) yeast (half a pack)
1.5 tsp salt
50g (2oz) cold, grated butter
50g (2oz) spelt or wholemeal flour
400ml (14 fl oz) lukewarm water
700–800g (1½ –1¾lb) wheat flour
Pesto to taste
A generous cupful (250ml) of coarsely grated Parmesan cheese
30 chopped olives

1 Stir the yeast, salt, grated butter and spelt or wholemeal flour into the lukewarm water.
2 Add the flour gradually and knead into a smooth dough.
3 Cover the dough bowl with cling film and let the dough rise until doubled in size.
4 Roll the dough out to approximately 40 x 60cm (16 x 24in) on a floured surface.
5 Spread a thin layer of pesto over the whole surface of the dough and sprinkle with the Parmesan cheese and chopped olives.

6 Roll the dough up like a Swiss roll and cut 3cm (1¼in) slices.
7 Divide the slices on a baking tray covered with baking paper and put them aside to rise again for approximately 30 minutes.
8 Bake the buns in a preheated oven for approximately 15 minutes at 230°C (gas mark 8 or 450°F).